"Victor Clevenger is a writer whose work I genuinely get excited to read. He has a unique voice that he seamlessly reinvents time and time again, that always remains Clevenger. *Every Angel in Heaven is a Hopscotch Champion* is collection of over 300 selected poems from out-of-print releases spanning 2016 - 2020. Buy this book."

-Tohm Bakelas, poet, editor of Between Shadows Press

I0518895

"Reading Victor Clevenger's *Every Angel in Heaven is a Hopscotch Champion* I was forced to re-examine what I thought I knew about his work. The words between these pages aren't weary, but speak to the staying power of childhood nostalgia and the growing pains we all go through well into middle age and beyond. This collection is Clevenger at his most thoughtful, his most personal, just like life--you never know what's just around the corner or the next page. Opening this book is like opening your mind to the possibilities you thought were behind you, drawing the curtains of your mind, and letting a little sunshine wash over your heart."

- John Dorsey, author of *Pocatello Wildflower*

"The fresh voice of an old school poet cruising the soft light of an empty corner just before the crushing ace high flush of first light blows thru the leaves of your one true love, this dawn explosion giving rise to the music of a fearless young lion coming home again."

- S.A. Griffin, author of *Pandemic Soul Music*

"Reading Victor Clevenger is like stepping into a pair of well-worn, but still comfortable shoes; they might not be what's in fashion, but they'll take you where you need to be. His poems are snapshots into the hearts of the lives of us all. With great tenderness, but also (sometimes ruthlessly) without apology, this collection is Clevenger at his finest, truest, and most devastatingly real."

> - James Benger, author of *From the Back,* and founder of the online workshop *365 Poems in 365 Days*

"As Michaelangelo saw the angel in the marble and carved until it was set free, Clevenger sculpts the hard jagged stuff of this world into cottony fabric and warm yielding flesh. He shapes a series of astonishing moments from an immense block of stone the size of his lifetime, chipping away until the poetry wastes not a word. With the precision of a surgeon, Victor draws not only the blood from rock but brings out tears and breath."

> - Jonathan S Baker, author of *Obituaries* and co-author of *Centaur*

"With tough guy bravery, heart that will sweeten your brew, and uninhibited sexiness, *Every Angel in Heaven is a Hopscotch Champion* is a full entree of poetry. The unpredictability of life shifts from something lonely to something beautiful with the additions of friends, children, and lovers. This collection is founded on the wisdom that we each carry the sunlight of hope."

> - Linzi Garcia, author of *Thank You*

Every Angel in Heaven is a Hopscotch Champion

Selected Poems [2016-2020]
Victor Clevenger

Spartan Press

Spartan Press

Kansas City, MO

spartanpress.com

Copyright © Victor Clevenger, 2024

First Edition: 1 3 5 7 9 10 8 6 4 2

ISBN: 978-1-958182-83-3

LCCN: 2024944323

Cover photo: Jason Baldinger

Author photo: Victor Clevenger

Acknowledgments

The selected poems gathered for this collection have previously appeared in various forms in the following books published between 2016 - 2020: *In All These Naked Pictures Of Us* (IP), *Come Here* (Least Bittern Books), *The More Exciting Side Of Death* (Epic Rites Press), *SoulWhore* (Svensk Apache Press), *Congenital Pipe Dreams* (Spartan Press), *Sandpaper Lovin'* (Crisis Chronicles Press), *Tom Farris is My Brother* (CWP Collective Press), *Her Bastard Soul* (Epic Rites Press), *Ginger Roots Are Best Taken Orally* (with Tom Farris, EMP), *A Finger in the Hornets' Nest* (Red Flag Press), *On The Tip Of Our Tongues* (Analog Submission Press), *Corned Beef Hash by Candlelight* (Luchador Press), *Dog Park 2* (River Dog), *Low-Flying Birds* (River Dog), *A Walk Down Mammary Lane* (Analog Submission Press), *The Ghosts of Our Words Will be Heroes in Hell* (with John Dorsey, Jason Ryberg, & Damian Rucci, OAC Books).

I want to thank all the editors who originally published these books, as well as all the editors where individual poems may have previously appeared online or in anthologies: *The Gasconade Review, As It Ought To Be Magazine, Lady Chaos Press, Dead Snakes.com, Rat's Ass Review, UFO Gigolo, BoySlut Magazine, Elephant, NEAT, Eleventh Transmission, Least Bittern Books, Bad Acid Inc., Your One Phone Call, Sediments Literary Arts Journal, 48th Street Press Broadside Series, Poetry Pacific, Spartan Press, Crisis Chronicles Press, NightBallet Press, Rose of Sharon Press, Blue Hour, Ramingo's Porch, Apache Poetry Blog, Misfit Magazine, Trailer Park Quarterly, Ted Ate America 5, 365 Poems Anthology, Horror Sleaze Trash, San Pedro River Review, Thimble Lit Magazine, Mad Swirl, Punch Drunk Press, Pski's Porch: Resurrection of a Sunflower, Cyberwit.net, Holy&intoxicated Publications, Varnish Journal, Shine Runner Press, 13 Myna Birds, Yellow Chair Review, Zombie Logic Review,* & *The Dope Fiend Daily.*

Table of Contents

A special thank you & much love to Crissy &
the Youngsters, John Dorsey, Jason Baldinger, Jason
Ryberg, Mark McClane, Tony Hayden, The Osage Arts
Community, S.A. Griffin & Lorraine Perrotta, John
Burroughs, Dianne Borsenik, Rebecca Schumejda,
Mike & Eva West, Curtis Hayes, Wendy Rainey,
Chase Dimock, Mj Taylor, Allison Knightly, John
Macker, Nikki Allen, Tohm Bakelas, Cord Moreski,
Scott Laudati, Danny D. Ford, Mark Anthony Pearce,
Damian Rucci, Rebecca Webber, Jonathan Baker,
Jake St. John, Marc Burseke, Ed & Eva Gehlert, Paul
& Reverie Koniecki, Tom Farris, Carlos & Opalina
Salas, Nadia Arioli, Shawn Pavey, James Benger, Scot
D. Young, Adrian Lime, Jonie McIntire, Bob Phillips,
Kerry Trautman, John Walz, Chris Knopp, Joseph
Fulkerson, Nathaniel Stolte, Ray Swaney, Bree, Wesley
Scott McMasters, , Ezhno Martin, Heather Minette,
Linzi Garcia, Tim Tarkelly, & John Clayton.

I remember trying to figure things out—(life)—trying to get it all down to something basic—and ending up with nothing. Except a dizzy head.

— Joe Brainard

Every Angel in Heaven
is a Hopscotch Champion

A Year 2020 Mindset

standing on
our front steps

i catch
falling rain
in my hands

let it spill over
onto concrete

if it was
red wine

i'd put it
up to
my mouth
& sip it

until the sky
emptied

its very
last bottle

Peeping Back at the Thunder's Growl

for John Dorsey

walking on bone-dry ground
beneath a low brown cherry moon

feeling cooped up
from a world once known

you dream your body a bird at nighttime

waiting on the rain to fall like the blood

of all those better days

Tuesday Night in July

garbage can sat in the dark

neighbor said yesterday that he tossed
two chickens in there after his dog
had attacked & killed them

smelled like death's love bed
as i tossed my sack in on top

flies rose above
& then settled back in

to climb all over each other
in hot wet ecstasy

& it would have been
a downright beautiful thing

if it wasn't

absolutely disgusting

Poem for Graceyn

at times the damn tooth fairy forgets
to stop in & drop a quarter
while you are sleeping

it's much more common
than you would think

after all   she's not perfect

so much like your teeth
in their current state

Hot Things Are Just Cold Things with Heat

you say love
a strange   strange thing

i say it's like a frank standford poem

beautiful & wanting more

like small doves in stew pots
without vegetables

when starving
i give you my portion

& watch you smile

picking through tiny bones
like diamonds scattered

on a paper plate

Hard-Bitten

my face has always been the remnant
of a ravished battlefield
when i was a young man
i washed my face thirty times one day
trying to remove its structure
i was never able to remove it
it remained   it went nowhere
i was forced to wear it
i still wear it
it's tough   it's nude
& tough nude is not for faces like mine—
tough nude is for young lovers
drinking champagne on rooftops
tough nude is for people in twenty-dollar magazines
that i never buy
i just look at the covers
& thumb through the pages
while wondering how you have ever
found the courage
to kiss me with your eyes open
in the brightest light
of the nighttime

Chorus of a Death Song

when i was young
i tried to rescue a small bird
that had been abandoned
put it in a shoebox in my bedroom
& it lived for only six days
crooning a version
of the very same song that
these hatchling robins are singing right now
from the belly   all sitting against
a ground level window
the   chorus   of   a   death   song
echoing off a weathered board
affixed with rusty nails to fill a void
when the stained glass shattered years ago
a young jesus was never resurrected
passing by   i listen to them
& look around as they go silent
shhhh . . .
a yellow cat with hungry eyes
creeps slowly around a bush
not ten feet from the nest
& their mother will return soon
to sing
that familiar song
all afternoon

Poem for Kevin Ridgeway

those who utterly understand
that each human emotion
has its own color

will be able to see
all the amazing things made
with a single brushstroke
of black

High Above Powerlines

the birds who sing in the sky
only know you from a great distance

so they cannot see the fourteen cuts
from a razor blade still weeping
from your thighs like raindrops
down exit signs

or the word goodbye
that you have written on the soles
of both your shoes

they wish they could
but they cannot

they just sing in the sky

their whistles
one day turning into ghost songs

for your mother's daughter

After the Duck's Head Falls

after the duck's head falls
to the swing of a hatchet
& blood washes down
into the dirt's cracks
like thirsty mouths begging

i think about those quacks
that i'd heard for many months
before & wonder
how far their sound
actually traveled through hot air

did they reach that moment
where ghosts & last embers
of yesterday's stars
heard them fade crackle pop
into non-existence

or are they still there floating endlessly

silent in protest

brushing up against my cheeks
like a kiss

The Last Supper

the sun turns its back on us daily
turns a blind eye to it all

vultures fall to the ground to feast
without remorse

knowing that

while resting against filthy rib bones
a heart does not grow
like a wildflower
in blood

Poem for My Grandson

congress impeached the president
just hours before your mother
gave birth to you

it's a fact that you
weren't the only red eyes crying
that night   & i

may have just been the happiest
man in town

Southern Un-Hospitality

with the stench of inherited hate
& liquor on their breath

santiago doesn't reply to the provoking

he just lets them say what they want
in the drive-thru lane
because he has only worked
the milkshake machine behind the counter
for three days & he doesn't want
any trouble from the people
in this 'merican city

yet santiago isn't a bad dude
& he doesn't make the milkshakes
taste any different than if
an american had made them
but he's not american

just a good guy lumped into a group
of bad hombres

who have learned first-hand
that there is nothing sweet
about the ignorant tooth
that bites down on the rib bones
of nationalism

2 Lovers on South Aiken Avenue

kissing each other with mouths open wide
mashed together bodies leaning
against a telephone pole

near the closed day care center
on the corner

your hands up her shirt
& hers up yours

i'm certain that you have no clue i'm even there
waking up at 3a.m. on the concrete step
across the street half-hungover
& watching you

thinking about
how i do not feel like a creep

because there is not one single star
in the sky that is dead
& falling

they're all high & holding

watching you two
lust rub & dance

to any pittsburgh street sound
that resembles
a tune

What I Didn't Know While Eating Bacon in Jeannette, Pennsylvania

that in only a few short hours
while driving through heavy rain
at sixty miles-per-hour
down a dark illinois hwy
coming home
we'd see at the end of two lusterless headlights
a dead dog lying
in the middle of the road
naturally
it in a motionless state showed
that that we were not the first car to pass by
& in the rearview mirror i could see
that we were not going to be
the last car to pass by either
we were just going to be one of many
passing right through the middle
of a horrible situation
that night
i thought about every dead dog
i'd ever buried
now sitting on wooden stools
somewhere beyond the living
ordering up the first round
for that poor wet bastard's
first night of many
chasing the stars like bones
broken & tossed across
constellations

Three Minutes Late & Out of Luck

rolling slow through a kfc parking lot
in pryor, oklahoma
a young dark-haired girl eating a fried
chicken leg on the other side
of the drive-thru window tells us
we're three minutes late & out of luck
when we try to order food at 10:03 p.m.
you've got to be kidding me!
her compassion like coleslaw's complex
always rejected   horrible
our stomachs now growling like stray dogs
lost in an unfamiliar neighborhood
of vegans   & trash dumpsters
with padlocks

The Color of a Deep Depression

watching the sky fall in thick pieces

like broken blue bricks
or tiny paint chips picked from
a van gogh canvas

who's the monster
that would destroy such masterpieces

have you ever heard it said that
we are all masterpieces

our individuality birthed
by strokes of colored brushes
in the finger pinch
of a powerful someone
splitting their soul in a solarium

it's 9:55 this morning

& i sit here imagining the color
that the water has turned into

all the brushes that created us
sitting in a cracked glass jar on a
windowsill in the sun

i bet it's murky

the color of a deep depression
plummeting down
like raindrops on the thirsty

& that makes sense to me

because most days i feel buried in the dirt
up to the notch in my neck

looking towards the sky
& just taking

what is being given

Lost Man's Candle

standing at the end of a cold day
we think about how it is always here
in some form good for a glow
hanging from a rope
tied to a breeze

it's a lost man's candle
the moon

creating the dull between the trees
branch's shadows like arms reaching out
for a waist to grasp in dance
& we're near

but there is no melody left in our breath
tonight   & there is no whistle
from the lips of the wind either

just the random cries of wild animals
that we've all heard
a thousand times before

as we stood there like fools

too fucking stubborn
to just find

a good path back home

Poem for My Hometown (or, An Abusive Relationship)

your head covered with a white quilt

like a ghost looking off into the distance
i struggle to recognize you anymore

i want to wrap my arms around you, hamilton
& talk like we used to

but you won't reply
because you've let them stitch
your lips shut

for that all mighty dollar
i'm certain that your legs are next

because everyone knows that a nest of hornets
can never grow stronger
if you destroy their existence
right now

Poem for Lora

deep down inside i was secretly prepared for the
reality that our relationship was just another
youngster romance

a couple of crazy kids in the late summer of '96
listening to cake

& going the distance

A Poem About Rose Bushes

independent at seventeen years old
pocketing six-dollars-n-hour
painting bedroom walls
on a saturday afternoon
& afterwards
before the streetlight's flicker
i was drunk again
drifting into a sunday morning
six o'clock awakening
lying on a living room floor
near a window seat
in a low-income housing complex
with an older woman
who shook my shoulder
then led me to a back bedroom
where we ended naked
under heavy covers
sleeping until eleven

that was the first time with her
a month into my senior year
of high school

two weeks removed
from my father's house
& learning
that with nothing to show
the true colors of the petals to come
it's a gamble

to take only a piece of the root
& bury it with assumptions

because twenty-two years ago
i would have sworn to you
that i was growing
a marilyn monroe rose with her
when honestly
i grew nothing more
than a wilted memory lane

Poem for Carlie & Cassie Clevenger

you are both fruit that has finally fallen
& rolled a good distance away
from your mother's tree
   i'm sure
that the orchards in your future will now
be beautiful

Clevenger Painting

when piccard & jones had just flown
the first balloon non-stop around the world
i was working seven days a week
on a job site painting new homes
for happy people
with more money than i had
my fingernails stained with minwax
puritan pine & early american
a mixture of shit
smeared on every set of oak cabinets
in platte county missouri spring 1999
nostrils full of hi-build lacquer & dust
ears buzzing huffing stoned
during my lunch breaks talking to tommy
who had spiked hair & a neck tattoo
a hired hand dating my cousin tonya
after he'd done some time in the penitentiary
& i was seven months into my first marriage
at that point working for the family business
so we would joke about how i was doing
a double bit of hard time myself
shackled & chained
without the balls & keys to break free
but quite often i'd tell myself
four months past my turning nineteen
that i refuse to stroke myself into a corner
day after day with a thin bristled brush
that had dried up years ago
with someone else's dull
earth toned dreams

I am Legend (or, Poem About Helping My Children Build Valentine's Day Boxes)

the only gun that i own shoots staples
in dreams
i am will smith
navigating through a paper heart
apocalypse

Poem for Madi

in a salina ihop
the first thing i notice is your
long legs

standing on your tippy toes
i bet you can see over the nighttime
into tomorrow

how beautiful
the sound of a distant moan

clouds kissing your neck every night
like a lover

Jay

on a friday just before lunch
you were arrested by the state police
for child pornography
& more

i wonder if they were gentle with you
or if they threatened you
with harm if you ever told a soul
about what they were getting ready
to do to you . . .

the things that change a person forever

Jay #2

after one night in jail
you called michelle
& asked her
to send you money

but she told you no
& to never call again

& i love her
for being strong

you swore to her
that your daughter wasn't
a victim of your actions

goddamn jay

do you realize how stupid
you sound

desperate words rushing
out your mouth like water
through a hole in the bottom
of a boat

that you've packed
your future onto

Jay #3

you went from working in a prison
with us every day

to living in one

walking that razor's edge
& paying rent

with your sins

Jay #4

making excuses as to what
led you down that dark path
to where twelve-year-old girls
became your thing

you blame your mental health

for the reason young girls
argue with their friends
that monsters
are real

Jay #5

sometimes jay
there are no more secrets to hide

some men are nothing more
than wet bones waiting
for the day to be dropped into a hole

& i hope

that your beautiful daughter grows up
with a different
last name

Favorite Couch at the Dorsey Hotel

this couch is fearless
bones once new & shiny
in the summer of '77

when the son of sam still strutted
the streets of queens

this couch is fearless
been this way for forty-two years
with cushions that have sworn to men
they could take a .44 caliber bullet
in the kisser

hot hole burnt through
& through

spit out white stuffing like teeth
into the palm of their hands
before putting it all
into a zipper pocket to share
in stories later

it's craziness
mixed with an unforgettable
scent of cocky

that most can overlook
including me

spread out on top of her
under a plush blanket
with a book of yi sha poems
across my chest

i too
for a moment feel fearless

in my mind
watching an episode of tomorrow play
dancing in the darkness
of tonight

Southern Missouri Hindsight Proverb

on a rusted-out condom vending machine
that hangs on a wall in a bathroom
at a small gas station off highway 67

someone has written

Your Daddy Should Have Bought One Of These

Reggie & The Milkman

in the living room
reggie drunk preaches to the milkman
about living his best life

tells him to get rid
of any & all hate inside of himself

that's tearing at the walls
of his stomach

because one day it may rip open

& how awful would that feel
to have your guts crashing down
to the ground around your bare feet

like a paper sack full of shit
that's been lit on fire

by the flame
of your own bad decisions

Tenderloins

reggie tells the milkman
that passion is multi-use seasoning
sprinkled on with best guesses
& that   it tastes savory
in the early morning
when you're still stoned &
chewing on the consequences
of having sex in a public place
with someone just as stoned & hungry
as you are

Bank Robber Blues

one afternoon   john prine sang a song
his rich soul jumping out
a cell phone speaker

my son laughed when he said
dead peckerhead

what are you going to do when you get to heaven?

told him i do not know   said maybe
heaven is place for better men than me

we talked about bullshit successes & failures
right up until the last swallow of high life

& i ended the conversation

you're just a young man learning
an old man's lesson:

even when you take matters
into your own hands
you are not always going to blow
the vault door off the hinges

just be thankful
you have still got the dynamite

to try again another day

Thursday Evening in September

for nothing more
than to close an open window
i rushed into the first room on the left
with a bust-down-a-door
cop mentality

& his sudden search for concealment

reminded me why
it's always best to knock first
& wait for him to finish twisting the knob
before entering the room with caution

it doesn't always take a gunshot
or a slice from a sharp blade
to leave a scar

sometimes

it's just a hard object
gripped by a hand

A Solid 630

moving through the air like a silver dollar
quick flipped from the tip of a thumbnail

shouting 720 but falling 90 short

he says it's okay
as he climbs again & again just to leap

from the top turnbuckle of his dreams

down onto the solid ground
of reality

Milkman's Mustache

i offer him a razor for the first time

he declines it
like a thirsty hound from hell
when offered holy water

turning his head from side to side
in front of a bathroom mirror

admiring something that looks quite fragile in its infancy

like spiderwebs the color of rust
that spell out the word masculinity
in a thin font stretched

across his cracked lips

Milkman's Moves

i'm certain that
he's yet to touch a girlfriend's nipple

but the day is coming

goddamn

his life
is getting good

Dirty Castle Weekend

spotting a young waitress at the dinner belle
the milkman confessed that she
was out of his league
that she was far too beautiful for him
to even talk to
that she was probably seventeen or eighteen
& as she approached the table
with a notepad & pencil
he nervously moved about his seat
saying
i'll take the outlaw with fries
knowing damn well
that any hot sauce they smothered
that chicken breast in
could never make him sweat as much
as whispering
those six words
to her

The Java Break Incident

unknowingly protecting the prey from a predator

when the milkman stole all of linzi's attention
that night in lawrence, kansas
it really did a number on jameson

but don't worry milkman   you were young
& besides

there were thirteen other times before that one
that his failures resulted in a suicide attempt

& those

had nothing to do with you

$5.00 Wok

a $5.00 wok was a helluva steal
an after christmas deal

sitting over the flame
for the first time
on new year's morning

it's the milkman's birthday breakfast

three pounds of pork sausage
browned crumbled glistening in grease

i antique it with flour
stir it until coated

reach over
take the eggs off the griddle

biscuits out the oven

grab the milk &
dump two cups on the meat

goddammit!

white liquid hit the bottom
& as soon as the plastic spoon
made its first clockwise rotation
the black coating on the pan

floated in flakes to the top
goddammit!

black flakes now bigger
than sausage crumbles

i call the milkman to the kitchen
& show him the gravy

whatcha gonna do he asks
& i think about it

then tell him
it's like the ol'sayings

. . . . like a turd in a punchbowl
                    or
. . . . like a trump in the white house

some things just aren't salvageable

so i guess

we throw it out

& begin again

Nostalgia

summer
was suggestively better
back when we knew no laws of nature
& could easily kiss the neck
of a lightning bolt

The Wild

unraveling the bird
from the bush

a stone whispers
a confused language

into the ear
of an unraveling town

To Break or Barter

with no white flag
to spread over flesh

we slither

under the nose of
            hope

Behind the Door

what good is my mouth for dancing
like chickens in a kitchen

or angels

on the curve of a heart

Inner Nature

i'm sure it's not
a crime
but my father
never said that
an all-consuming
irrational love
has a distinctive
intensity
deliberately crafted
under the pressure
of a short duration

For the Flare of Rich Men's Daughters

my friend is instantly desperate
for destiny to suddenly drag
his fluttering life around
a curve

All Afternoon

deciding that death
is a broken
down love machine

i fumble
with getting all

or nothing

at the bar

Full of Magic

low-flying birds
see all the love fiends

down there in streetcars kissing

while needles

fall out of haystacks

Nourish

thrusting flesh thru flesh
we enter each other

holy angel

i bring yr flowers
wetness

The Situation

my white legs are not
her cool california dreams

dancing around
with sexual energy

i feel a rush of dumb
across my body

& she laughs

with tears in her eyes

Wish You Were Here Too

my love hand   loving myself off
over a sink somewhere in kansas city

the sun flashes

miles above my tremors

Masochism

you left a hitting stick

& your red pants on a chair
in the living room

i suffer
shouting

i never really wanted it to go down this way

White Silence

snow gliding
down a wooden windowframe

i quiver

with all the secrets
i have left

in the ripples

Vaccine

we seem
doomed

smell like
worry

but still dream nightly

of magic

Through All the Bullshit in the World

this morning
someone is singing your ghost song
into the wind

& the mountains

pile high with love

Poem for My Grandson #2

on a sidewalk stone hard hotel mattress
in farmington, missouri   i'm alone again
like sunshine at midnight never seen
traveling job blues   & in-betweens
sitting with silver rum & tonic water
in two paper cups reading
the courtyard poems by frank t. rios when
at 10:19pm your mother sent a message
to my telephone   a photograph
of you in dim lamplight
half stewed on milk & dreaming
a smile in your sleep like joy's plush blanket
drug across your bare feet   comfort
at the end of a day
when falling ice outside conspired
to hold our existence hostage
our flesh our bones our breath
captured by interior walls
& restrained by threads unseen
but neither we cried out
or shouted
for help   in fact
in that photograph you looked as happy
& content as my heart
at that very moment sending
a reply message back to your mother
at 10:20pm
i told her thank you
for thinking
about me too

Street Preacher

in grand junction, colorado
a drunk man stands in a parking lot
shouting through the windows at us
about making bad choices
as the waitress takes our order
we turn our head
ignore him & he leaves
after we're served
& take our first bites
in collective disgust we know
that he meant no harm
that he'd stumbled upon us in peace
to preach under the influence
to four damned idiots
who all ordered hamburgers
at a denny's

Contortionism

for Anna Tivel

if a man or woman could press their bones flat
into dust & magic   to be folded sharply
into a paper airplane   they would do it
underneath any dark chandelier

before begging the sun to rise tomorrow
   morning
over the alleyways in slow motion

for satisfaction

as they float out of control on a breeze

that began with every gentle exhale
between the words that you sang tonight

Christian Ready for the Fire

with his hair parted
slicked to the right like mine
he orders the kung pow chicken
drizzles sriracha for good measure
then forks a bite

that afternoon at the china restaurant
on old highway 24
i watch my son push through the pain
just to be like his old man

on the drive home
i tell him just wait
because the feeling isn't over

he says   ugh
i know
all things that enter
must pass through

you're right   i reassure him

each morning
you'll sit on the cold seat
reflecting on decisions you've made

& some won't feel good

but you'll wipe your ass clean
stand up

wash your hands
look in the mirror
& consider yourself lucky

to still be producing
& breathing the stink

because you're alive

& understand
that the dead

can no longer do

what you

can do

Mother's Day Mayhem

some nights
call for a few beers
& shots of rum come breakfast time
it's those same kind of nights
when i think about you
more than myself
you sitting at home
swallowing coffee & worry
me standing
in intense silence
under a moon that has one eye closed
with uncertainty
we both listen & wait
for the madhouse
to exhale its final breath
& be gone
this morning
i told you
that if broken glass could be melted into hope
i had walked over enough last night to know
that things are going to be okay
but that's fantasy
& as we laughed together
you passed the bacon
i tipped the bottle

Our Living

poor

was pain
to you & i

but when the
children were

young

they were
none the
wiser

& that was
a success we
accomplished
together

Downtime in Iraq

i heard stories
that the madman had
the most beautiful creatures
living somewhere within those waters
so every other day before breakfast
i would tie a string to a tree
throw sweet bagels attached to fishing hooks
into the death-pool-drainage lake
that trickled slowly
like lanced lesions from
the spread wide thighs
of the mighty tigris
after weeks waiting
i finally hooked the jawbone of something beautiful
struggled with its resistance
but eventually gained surrender
holding it in my homesick hands
i almost felt the urge to cry
i remember telling myself
don't do it   &   toughen up
who cries during wars anyway
with the urge growing stronger
i released the fish   &
stared straight into the sun without glasses
just to have an excuse
i wasn't tough enough to hold back tears
but i found ways around it
we all did   & i'm sure
we all still do

Behind Battle Lines & Bars

for matt borczon

swallowing hard
to the slow tick of a clock
the sky gets dark
when ghosts wrap thin films
of yesterdays
around your eyes
a reminder that
the greatest war
a man will wage
will not be
against his enemies
it will be against himself
the human mind
will always be a battlefield
filled with images
of hell
you learn
the trick is
to lift the sun by strings
tied to your footsteps
while running forward with hope
towards the radio transmissions
of a better tomorrow

Sharing the Ghosts of Yesterdays

nosediving deep into the depths
of a warm reassurance
saying
you once had slipped
from great heights
& got stuck in a moment

where your side was ripped open
by a crooked nail

& at first the blood ran down softly
like the tone of a whisper
but it built up quickly
to an intoxicating level of fear

that more demons would be summoned
than angels

to help sing the chorus

of just another sad swan song about falling
from the heavens

too many times

to walk away without scars

A Poem Written after Pulling Memoirs of a
Street Poet off the Shelf on the Night That
I Heard Frankie Died

grasping heartbeats
through skin
&
holding firm
like trapping a bee

between cupped hands
& breasts

intrigued

by how it feels

harmless

Sleeping With My Muse

like every frank t. rios
page set ablaze
i want you to wake me
from my dreams
on fire
all hours of the day
i want you to dance like
smoke through my skin layers
as i grasp to hold you in
i want you to stain
my fingertips permanent
like how ink bleeds
into the fibers of paper
i want you to leave your mark
on me
leave me no doubts
that you
        are the reason
we burn

Looking Through a Telescope

for mick guffan

craters in the surface of the moon

deep enough to hide
the secrets of our existence in

deep enough to hide
a thousand handfuls of pills in

i wonder

how many secrets
& how many pills would get swallowed

on lonely nights

before your black sky turned tangerine

Jelly Jar

i remember her walking
across cold wooden floorboards
towards a kitchen sink
where a jelly jar sat half-full of water

she only stopped long enough
to take a sip
but as she sat it back down   unleveled
it fell & shattered into pieces

holding her hand up
as if to say   nobody move
she started singing a patsy cline song
as she swept broken pieces of glass
into an old dustpan

this was the first time
that i'd heard her sing a sad song
but as i grew older & heard the stories
of the sudden shoves down stairs
the heartache   & her black-eye nights

it made sense to me
as to why this first time
wasn't the last time

In This Room

in the middle of the afternoon from a great distance
the sun is only a few inches wide
it's small

sitting on the ledge
near a window that we call cold
is a dying cactus

dirt dry & dreaming of better days

you say   it's like standing over a deathbed
we have to show it that we care
& the best thing that we can probably do
is to touch it

give it a real good loving embrace with our fingers
& our palms

but we can't shout

to make this all seem sincere

we just have to take the pain—

don't we

Poem for Blake McIntyre

long after the chalked hash marks
have washed away
with all the youthful dreams
of superstardom

& the friday night lights
have been shut out early enough
to catch just enough shuteye
to make it through another weekend shift
at the job

trying to earn enough money
to make ends meet in these depressed days
is no easy feat

you tell everyone
that will listen
to trust you

that the responsibility of adulthood

is no pancake platter at jerry's diner

The Army Has Invaded: Poem #1

sound the trumpets   ring the bells
in step a whole platoon curves around a peach pit
half-smoked joint lying in an ashtray
another day another ant parade
sweetly stoned & graceful
how long you plan on staying
i ask without receiving a reply
i learn   they don't give two-shits about me

The Army Has Invaded: Poem #2

march along march strong
marching soldiers march
nine black ants making their way up the side
of a cup
two days old
they won't listen   spoiled milk mission
it's not going to be sweet
march along march strong
marching soldiers march
i turn the kitchen light out & say   good luck
imagining their wives waiting at home
holding tiny heart-shaped lockets in their hands

The Army Has Invaded: Poem #3

i tell one of the ants that has strayed away
that he is probably safe
that he's far too small to have to worry
about someone
shooting him with a bullet
i wish i could say the same to my children
monday thru friday
when i give them their lunch money

The Army Has Invaded: Poem #4

cleaning up dried kool-aid by the coffee pot
graceyn says these ants are brave
or stupid   & i agree with her
either way you look at it though
the army is two-hundred strong tonight
clinging to a toaster they've turned into a foxhole
taking turns sleeping
with sugared mandibles
& pride
we thought about looking for the queen
but didn't really know what was appropriate to do
if we found her

The Army Has Invaded: Poem #5

it's ferlinghetti's birthday &
the youth of a nation shout in the streets
nobody should have to worry while falling
   asleep
but i wake with the soldiers
crawling on the lens of my eyeglasses
picking them up off the nightstand
i use my finger to swat them away
& i'm sure they'll come back
another day   because of course
they're trained for the war
so it's far more enjoyable than the peace
i want you all gone goddammit   i tell them
just go home to your wives tonight
& make love
so tomorrow when the sun rises
we can all smile about our victories

Nobody Wants This Stink

forced down the throat
of a toilet bowl
yesterday
my morning shit
was peachy orange
not a bright peach
not a bright orange
a burnt color smeared on paper
the porcelain refused
to swallow it voluntarily
i felt guilty
walking back into the room
with a plunger
in my hand
like i worked for
fox news

Ghosts on Crouch St.

death blows
down my street
from the south

making scratching sounds
against the asphalt

i wonder how long
these naked trees
will grieve
their children

lying
in the cracks
against the curbs
again

Birthday Séance Haiku

somewhere ghosts of good men
lick their sweet lips
as john dorsey eats his pie

Thirty Years

one small foot leads the other in a race
across childhood memories slowly
a growing shadow casts around a corner
looking like a crooked smile   familiar
gathered honeybees on the front porch screen
makes a buzzing sound like hair clippers
gliding through summer's growth
she squeezes wooden clothespins
between the thumb & fingers
whistles the best that she can
when she's done
the lines sag under the weight
let's go
climb in
make room
the devil went down to georgia
his favorite song on the radio
dashboard gauges useless   malfunctioned
but not a worry
a '79 thunderbird with the windows cracked
going to grandma's place
we were cruising at a speed of simplicity
that will never be felt again
that was thirty years ago
i light another cigarette
turn on don lemon   tonight
i am aging in a world of madness
falling apart
& all of my fears are the glue sticking the skin

to these bones
i am an arts-n-crafts project
from room to room
kissing my children goodnight
i wonder what
they will remember thirty years from now
on a thursday
in the month of april
when the sun slides out of the sky
& they're sitting all alone
at their kitchen tables

Off the Ledge like a Bird

at some point you must simply just leap
flames rising burning
rain falling drowning
wind blowing scattering
cold creeping freezing
dog dying elderly
kids crying argumentative
work daily draining
sun falling darkness
naked woman beautiful
loving woman distant
whiskey tonic drinking
eyes closing intoxication
alarm clock shouting
morning stomach nauseating
nauseating morning stomach
shouting alarm clock
intoxication eyes closing
drinking whiskey tonic
distant loving women
beautiful naked women
darkness falling sun
draining work daily
argumentative kids crying
elderly dog dying
freezing cold creeping
scattering wind blowing
drowning rain falling
burning flames rising
just leap at some point you must simply

Hush Kitty

eyes glow
staring out
from behind a curtain

as if to remind me
that she knows
all my dirty secrets

i call her over
to a food bowl
& give her anything she wants

because i know
that she definitely does not know
all my secrets

but i know
that she knows

more than most

A Horse He Called Beautiful

when all the rest would sleep
we would sit & i'd listen to stories
she'd laugh her way through some
grind her teeth with disgust during others
& look at the floor
when one of them shook loose a sad memory

i remember a story that she said was some
. . . . amazing disappearing acts & shit

said once it was bedtime
her husband would pull the sheets over himself
wait until she'd fallen asleep
& then vanish until the daylight came back again

said that in the late 40's
which would have been her early 20's
she spent a lot of time cussing the rooster's crow

knowing that she'd wake up lonely
& without the courage to set him straight
with the smack of her hand
against his dirty lying cheek

once he slipped back home over hills

half-sober sitting crooked in the saddle
on a long-legged horse

that she swore he loved far more than he loved her

My Mannequin at Barb's Books

we could have ruled the world together
she said

you made me feel a little less hollow inside

Pants at Easter

laughing at forgotten things
when remembered

wiping his hand across his knee   steve said
one time his pants were wrinkled

that's not very funny

he said   it gets better

lit a fire under a street lamp to smoke out bugs
hovering in the shouts of a hectic night

tried to stomp it out
& caught the pants on fire
jumped around
kicked off shoes
ripped away the pants
limped a few yards down the sidewalk
walked hunchbacked
looking at his bare legs
said the bugs were most likely laughing

his girlfriend was furious

she'd bought the pants at easter time
from her sister who wanted twenty dollars
& a burgundy pair of foster grant glasses for them

she paid ten & a chicken sandwich
told me not to tear holes in the knees
doing stupid shit

& i promised her i wouldn't

he started laughing again   this time
at a spoon on a table

& said i got another story to tell you

about an ice cream sandwich in troy, ohio

& a picture of a turtle
that i drew last march

One of Three Sides to a Story

that man has kissed his last opportunity goodbye
there's no way in hell
that my sweet ass will ever take him back
bent over at the waist
the girl beside a crow that's pecking at the
    ground
could tell anyone her problems
but today she chooses birds

my grandmother liked birds
had houses in the yard for them
they were neighbors   a decent kind of crowd
that didn't make you uneasy
early morning eating toast
in front of an open window
when focused on distant things
like a golden sun stretching for half a block
up one side of a building & down the other

as the crow flies   she stops talking
& i wonder how the man she was referring to
feels about any of this

Desire is a Box Built from Cherry Wood & Poplar

i figured you were probably expecting
   something
a bit fancier than a heart like a rusty nail

i was wrong

Beautiful Things Attract Beautiful Things

for belle

a shimmer lingers

it shows me
you're not a stranger
to the dust of burning stars

if you were to tell me
you could catch a hot one
in the palm of your hands

& hold it
like a passionate heartbeat
keeping it warm until the sun rises

i'd believe you

Peace Lilies

for west, mississippi & john dorsey

it's an eerie feeling

seeing how blood runs down a wilted petal
& drips onto the crippled stem
that grows up through a claimed crack
in the concrete

hearts beating slowly like
a bullet nervously tapped against a pistol's barrel

pissing in the wind & praying

that even the ghosts
of the toughest outlaws which guide us

suggest retreat

Found Poem: Woody's 50's Diner

please.........
whatever you do..
absolootly...
positively.....
do "not" look
into this hole

You Can't Escape What You Can't Escape

between sips of coffee
she tells me that it is not a bad job
fourteen dollars an hour with tips
& a meal mid-shift
but when she empties the ash trays
attached to the slot machines
the smell reminds her
of her mother's nightstand
when they lived in that hotel for a while
& even back then
she found it odd
that in the morning time
every man that her mother brought back
to have sex with
was introduced to her
as her uncle
like that was the solution
to make everything
that she had just experienced
seem better

Cold Love Poem

the key to prevent freezing
is to let love drip slowly

faucets attached to heart shaped pipes

i tell you

at six below zero in missouri
flesh is no more than a twin sheet
draped over bare bones

you agree

staring at the ceiling above us

we dream about crashing a car
into the sun

Wide-Eyed Wild

having sex on a couch once
like it was a cloud
inflated with some god's deep breath

she thought we were lovers dangling from the
   sun

asked if i could picture our shadows
stretched out for a thousand miles

asked if i thought it was odd
that our feet never seem to touch the rooftops
of this city that swallows us

i didn't think it was odd
   at all

just ran my fingertips through her hair
& let her talk beautiful to me

her lips parting were poems in themselves

words sharper than anything
cupid has ever pulled from
a quiver

 & aimed in my direction

Five Degrees in January

steam covers the bathroom mirror

i kiss her in the shower

waiting on the moon to melt
our frozen city

Tonight Like a Jukebox

you're standing in the shower
singing joan jett
i hate myself for loving you

i'm alone in the next room
singing the divinyls
i touch myself

together we finish with
bad reputation

& neither of us give a damn

our shared secrets are the dimes
dropped into the coin slots
of tomorrow's crooked smiles

In the Heat of a Moment

an earring was a star

falling to the floor

&

i secretly wished

for a baby to grow inside her

Jealousy is a Dirty Windshield

while traveling these highways
in the frozen darkness

she is every falling star

that boys wish upon

Corned Beef Hash by Candlelight

on the hottest day yet

i slowly pulled my fingers
out from between her legs

the tips wet like paint brushes

that had been dipped
into every single color of love

she'd created

a skip in the beat of a heart

that evening we ate corned beef hash
by candlelight

& agreed
that if you squinted your eyes
while looking into the flame

you could see something beautiful

Pine Scent & Marijuana

for heather hamilton

our '97 life in a rear-view
day skies were green
night skies
were hot-kaleidoscope-orgasms

we said together we'd love forever
because a day without loving
would be a day of certain misery
that we would never choose to wake to

i've lived twenty-years of days since then
all ones we said we'd never choose

& i have no idea
if they are miserable for you
i only know that there are still dark mornings
when i can feel a warm vibration
of you whispering words
into my ear

i wake quickly
alone   & imagine

our aged bodies
dangling like slivers of driftwood
from two beaded nooses
in this dreamcatcher
above my headboard

A Black Snake Moaning
Under a Shining Moon

love burning & chilling
distilling in a rib cage
drunken hearts make decisions
wake in the morning
devil's teeth clench
in reverence
alarm clock
killing us softly
long kiss
before goodbye
& a drive away

Sharing a Shower

she lathered her hair   scrubbed her skin
stepped to the back
i stepped into the water & did the same
rinsed first
reached down with my hands
grabbed my cheeks & spread them apart
leaned forward so that the water could rinse
my asshole clean
she laughed
i stopped rinsing & reached around her
grabbed her ass to spread her cheeks apart
then i laughed
she rinsed herself off
& we were done
afterwards
as we sat on the balcony
smoking   sharing red wine
i asked her
when she is at home tonight
with her husband & children
playing the role of fully committed
dinnertime discussing their afternoons
if i will cross her mind
when she says to them
that her day was uneventful
like any other day
these days

Like a Naked Woman in Sunshine

it's strange when the heat of the day
happens during the dark of the night
i'm always wide awake
lying there with my palm resting
between feminine thighs
wedged tight against the vagina of a woman
who intentionally sleeps with her body facing
away from me as i press yet another lonely hard-
on against her without success

i ask her in the morning as she wakes
did you hear the water dripping madly against the windows

she never hears it
or admits to hearing it

she climbs out of the bed first & shivers
while she gets dressed

i lie there alone for a moment watching her tug
english rose stockings up above her knees
   always
hopping on one foot & struggling with them

i soon climb out of the bed shivering too
& it is in this moment which i wonder
if other men at times have had these same kind
of nights like i have often had with her

sleepless & dreaming about someone else

Melting Roads

while navigating the ninth cloud
we shift through the gears
of the heart & the head

our secrets written on rusted street signs

we lose stability

slide sideways

into the sharp curves of a warm thirst

stopping at the driveway of desire
only to unlock the gate

From Father's Day to the First Frost

i believe in spirits
i cannot see

when two
voodoo dolls
are rubbed together

we both feel the tingle
in the flow of
our blood

Humming Champagne Supernova

the kids all sit oblivious in the kitchen
eating pancakes at the dinner table

we now in our late thirties
acting like 90's teens
sneaking down hallways

standing inside a bathroom during
a rainstorm

lightning outside
ripping through a cloud's bottoms
falling on trees like hot firework debris

crissy says   you better hurry up

as i pull my underwear down

like it was the first time with her
all over again

Morning's Hungover

too foolish
to accept that it could all be garbage

our love
will always be that pot of spaghetti
left out overnight on a stove

Bones Age with Each Breath

i wish i had an answer
wish i didn't have demons
didn't always feel like failing
i wish i didn't have a situation
was 22 again
i wish i was smarter
had gone to college
i wish i was living life
not letting life live me
i wish i had your heartbeat memorized
like a song by the national
wish i didn't feel everything closing
in on me   didn't always cry when i hurt
i wish that i could pick lilies for you
year round
walk to the kitchen right now
make you cinnamon rolls
i wish i was the earth to you
lick your armpits until you laugh
i wish i wasn't losing you to someone
that will never love you   i love you
i wish that my heart was actually an object
i could remove from my body
i would rip it out & give it to you without hesitation
as you sip your hot cup of vanilla biscotti
i light a cigarette
hazing the room like fog lifting over a cemetery
we've both seen
in a dream
but refuse to acknowledge

Insanity

flip an hour glass
o   r   o
  v   &   e   v
    e   v   &   e
     r   o   r

grains drop like eyelids
ice floats in rum
       then melts
dirty sheets
from last night's sex
pulled up to your
waist
       is lonely
       it is what it is
       it is
another
sunday morning
missing
you

Cold Rain Blues

it's 3:20 in the afternoon
where are you with lips like springtime
tongue like summer

on the front steps of your house
i'm just another wet songbird full of desire

singing for you
without a reply

Silent in Love

we see
birds of prey circling
the spaces above
our heads

today

my heart is like a
starving lion

waiting for you to say anything
with nourishment

Trying to Hold a Heart Hostage

we'd ditch a backseat
for a seventy-nine dollar room
on the second floor

have sex with law & order
playing in the background

after all those times
listening to the secrets
of how the cops catch 'em

you would have thought
i'd been well-schooled

a hardened criminal

who knew not to rely solely
on the promise of
i love you

as a restraining
mechanism

Sweet Chili Sauce on Cold Days When the Sun Stayed Asleep Until Noon

the times of eating hot wings
on hotel sheets together
have passed

sucking on the bones
of those memories

our souls will never starve to death

Strawberry Body Milk Poem

in an unfamiliar room
my right hand & hard-on smell delicious

Days on Lathrop St.

it's like i have just
swallowed the
goddamn sun

& chased it down
with a shot of brandy

i don't love this feeling
but then again
i don't hate it either

it's just what my insides
feel like when you
are near me

Sucking Blues Away

after months passed
feeling love sick

she sat on the edge
of the kitchen sink

offering her nipple
like the tip of a needle

that contained
the cure

Shoelaces

one morning you'll wake up late
be in a rush to
get out the door to punch a time clock
& find your
shoelaces tied together in many tight knots
you can't get undone

you'll shout & cuss me for doing such a thing
& i'll tell you that. it's. not. the end of the world

that it's just symbolism   that the laces
are you & i
that the undone knots are our embraces

then i'll tell of how it took me hours thinking about you
& of a way to show you that you're important to me

my best guess is that you'll say   how the fuck does
tying my shoelaces into knots show importance

& i'll tell you that i guess you have to think
outside the box a bit

but in all honesty   you have always been important to
me   but if i've ever made you doubt that

i'm sorry

& that i'll untie the knots for you   but only if you
promise to tie them back before you say
goodbye

excerpt from The Foxes

the distance black & quiet
 i'd fallen asleep on the
front porch when the rain turned into foxes
hanging from their neck were spoons & plates
i saw a thousand of them

a door underneath a flashing red sign would
    open &
they would all go inside   out of curiosity
people that were smoking pipes across the street
went inside too   all gathered in a very small space
they ate meatloaf

& laughed about something
that i really didn't find all that funny

*

one fox holds the door & they start to exit out
onto the sidewalk they're everywhere
stomach swollen   lips puckered sucking
    on straws
shoved in glasses of strawberry milkshakes
like it was a summer night stroll   1950s

the plates & forks are now gone   replaced by
boxing gloves that all have age to them
cracks filled with the peeled skin from chins of a
tougher generation

the smell of leather thick in the crowd
one spoke with the voice of my grandfather

said that in a white t-shirt
he's never look as cool as brando looks
but after
a sixer of pabst he really doesn't give a damn
because cool or not he's still just skin & bones
like every man   so that means a fair shot
at kicking his ass   & fair
is fair

*

a gun   someone shouted   A gun
a GUN   the words rang through the streets
all the fox eyes looked in many directions
i looked too

but never saw the gun before hearing
the first shot

if the shooter is good it happens this way

if the shooter is bad then they have failed
to watch as much american television
as the good shooter

*

the foxes now moving in a panic on the street
i blink   now i'm on a rooftop   confused
& looking over the edge
one shouted   JUMP   i shook my head no
one shouted   CHICKENSHIT
i shook my head no again

many more joined in the shouting & a few
started running   entering doors
which led to the roof where i was standing
   trapped
with a cup of black coffee spilling
onto my shoes

*

dropping the cup
they're going to throw you over   i told myself
i'll never let it happen
reaching into my pocket
pulling out a piece of twine wrapped tightly
between my fingers

stretched out between both hands

i really didn't know how easy it would be
to strangle a fox to death   but i remember
putting a viscous dog in a headlock once
when i was younger
because my best friend said
it was what men do to show the beasts
who is dominant

*

waiting   watching out into the distance
nothing appears there

i've no clue where they've gone

their charging with a madness has fooled me

like long slow kissing with a drunk married
   woman
convinced it's love   but when sober
it's clarified by her as making a mistake
& there's nothing more than friendship

it all makes me wonder
can you feel moments   of danger
without anger

*

looking back   over the edge
there are still foxes on the street

twine in my hands turns to ivy & i drop it
watch it twist a few times
like a fish on a hook

lands in a sink full of dirty dishes

*

looking around
no longer on a roof   now in a different place
things look familiar
this apartment is very similar
to the layout of the trailer house that i lived in
the year that my first daughter was born

lora walks quickly into the kitchen

my god   it has been so long
since you have been close enough
for me to touch you
          she says

have you seen all the foxes outside

for some reason i can't talk
i just stare at lora's teeth

they're still just as white as they were when
   we met
in the ninth grade

*

i want to tell her that they're lovely
so i smile showing mine   & point at them
with my finger

she doesn't understand what i'm doing

she hugs me

& i'm concerned that she thinks i've gone crazy

i don't know
maybe i have

An Acquired Taste

reggie tells me
that when he was young
he saw a woman stick the head of a snake
into her mouth & moan
like she was having an orgasm

says that when he sees a snake in the grass

he thinks about her

& about how some things
are just really

fucked up

I See You in Cities: Poem #1

for brittany

eating pussy for america
your back pockets stained with bourbon st filth
handing you a half empty beer can
you poured what remained slowly
into your mouth
your tongue quite tired
taking long trips in circles
spreading love's folds
a gift you give to a maddened world
the answer to the question i ask
you already know

how many licks does it take
to get to the center of human kindness

I See You in Cities: Poem #2

for brittany

out of darkness stumbling
beyond a beat
you've materialized again
shoulders draped in a white scarf
nobody in a crowd has a face
only you do
with a ginsberg book laid across my lap
i stare into your eyes
see ripples on the surface of wishing wells
you whisper & i believe your words to be true
hate is a finger that tickles too many in these times
it gets tougher daily to float on breezes
with love weighing you down
blue socks damp & stained with venice blvd
you wrapped your arms around my ribs
before stepping over the threshold
of my heart's front door & i've never had
a ghost inside me
quite as lovely

Two Haiku

it's not a diamond
you're stoned
holding a dog's tooth up to the sun

in winter
a junkie that dies in an alley
won't rot until spring

Four to Six

the worst part wasn't when she left him
it was when she never returned

& he had kept all the items she had left behind
sealed in a box under his bed   said that
he thinks about it all the time   yet

it hadn't been opened in eight months
confessed he had even saved
a bedsheet that was stained with
faded blood spots from her menstrual cycle

after we finished a second cup of coffee

he asked me   if you rate on a scale
from one to ten
how crazy do you think i am

Cheeking Haldol

she said their bodies stacked up
like snapped twigs in a ditch
dusted with the first frost
of '84

that saturday morning
daddy soaked the pile with kerosene
lit all seventeen dogs on fire
sang that kenny & dolly song
islands in the stream
as they burned

said some things
are not meant for a person to see
but i still see them

i used to see daddy's face
how it looked before
i pulled the trigger
but i don't see him much anymore

it's just the sight of those goddamn dogs

wet-tongued-spirits
licking me to sleep every night
in a corner

Pearl

eating a roast beef sandwich as she explains
how she wants to cut off a piece of her ear
& paint it the color of a pearl

so that she can toss it back into the sea
from high upon a rock cliff similar to one
her mother described to her as a little girl

i tell her   hope it all works out

listening to her talk
to her chew her meat & bread
to two cars pass by
to that voice inside me saying
how the pretty girls in this town all seem
to be crazy

when she asks   if the roles were reversed
& that silly little bitch had died first
. . . do you think that romeo
would have said   O happy dagger

Poem for Jameson Bayles

you were more like a 1990's emo song
than an inspirational hymn for young women

Poem for Kyra at 2 A.M.

lips painted the color of barbie's convertible
you sell corndogs
at a convenience store in nebraska

dreaming & convinced
that you'll never just settle
because your damn certain
that your ken is somewhere close

he's coming for you
with shoulders covered
in the dust of falling stars

each time
that a new big rig pulls onto the lot
you get a nervous feeling inside you

thinking
that this may be the day
that you finally get to run away to malibu

& show them
that thick thighs are beautiful too

With Ten Toes & an Extra Heartbeat
   inside You

you throw out rib bones
like boomerangs
beyond veins
the slow rolling rivers
that all meet
at the mouth of a heart

there's something special
about captured moments like this

guiding my fingertips against your skin
i traverse the stretch marks
that have materialized
like constellations spread across
the pale night sky
we dream beneath

Four Flights to Freedom

on her first night we laugh
at the cabinet doors that are missing their knobs

as sounds from a gay bar enter through a
broken window
& drag queens smoke cigarettes—

sharing gossip in the hallway
allison tells me she's excited to finally be
living alone

a single air mattress
inflated on the floor of her bedroom
attempts to provide separation
from the hardwood
as her tequila splashed lips blow kisses
that travel
on the summer winds
whispering impending departure

the only ghost that she senses in the room
sings a sinatra tune
about love

& nothing seems scary tonight

Meth Rock in His Pocket

my heart like a bone
laid in a woven basket like bread
ribs aged almost forty years
i know my fate
the feeling of being ripped open
by an animal's tooth doesn't sadden me anymore

bentley though
his heart's like a handful of water
falling upon the parched lips of all that follow
sometimes i just watch him
he looks like a red-haired jesus christ spreading love
in a city park

last night he asked me about his mother again
said he wished she'd just come back to see him
& i didn't know what to say
because i've never told him the truth
that four years ago she disappeared
while chasing a man with a meth rock
in his pocket
& that i never tried to stop her

because i knew better
than to wage a war that i'd never win

with all the demons she had inside of her

i would have had more success
lying on my back & trying to piss
on the side of the sun

My Best Friend

for reggie

live in a glass house
throw stones through the ceiling

swear they land like bombs
but don't detonate
just collect in the night sky
on ten squares chalked across a fantasy

now you say
every angel in heaven is a hopscotch champion

Graveyard Shift

come home at eight in the morning
stumble in
reggie is lying in the doorway
half his body inside
half is out
i ask if he had a rough night
he replies   it was a dream
he almost died
wonders if i have ever felt
that i was coming close to death
i tell him   once or twice
remind him of the failed suicide attempt in 2002
he asks if i called out for god
in the moment that i thought
it was surely all over
tell him   i didn't
he crawls the rest of the way inside
says he didn't either
says he called out for his father
like a scared child
who needed firm comforting
assured him that i knew that feeling
that on occasions
i had expressed that feeling myself
he says he's alive
it doesn't matter anymore
that he's going back to sleep
i tell him   g'night
sit down to take my boots off

kid's mom walks down the hallway
asks who i'm talking to
& if i'm hungry
i'm not
but i eat half a bagel anyway

On a Thursday

i finished a ten-hour shift painting houses
under a sun in summer
stumbled home to a kitchen that still smelled
like last night's greasy supper
nothing new

really just wanting to sit down
shit & then drown in a bathtub of saltwater
she wanted to have sex
sitting shirtless in a chair

it's good for a relationship
she said
yeah   i replied
still being in love is too

she didn't say another word that evening

when i finally joined her in bed
i dreamt that all the dogs from hell
had suddenly fallen down on the sidewalks
& turned into piles of sand
store owners came outside to scoop them all up
& poured them into hourglasses

when i woke i had a strange feeling in my chest
wasn't sure what it was
rolling across the bed
i kissed her on the shoulder

three months later we called it quits

Reggie's Advice During My 1st Marriage

they're stupid
but even flies eventually give up on dead things

& move on

Continued Quest for a John Dorsey Book

reggie laughed out loud
& told me good luck

when i said

i'd pay a couple hundred dollars
for sodomy

Reunion

monday evening
reggie's daughters came to visit

it had been six years
since he had last seen them

when they arrived he greeted them
they didn't speak

he flicked his tongue out & in quickly
to try & break the silence

they never cracked a smile
or made eye contact

he looked back at me for advice
his eyes open glassy
desperation

i don't know
that i'd ever seen that side of him

like blood
after a bullet enters

small pieces of his toughness
dripped down his forehead
slowly

Forced Sober

days are getting rougher
miles growing greater
distance is the demon's chin i swing at

knockout punches in dreams
each time forget how it feels to fight
palm fist feet elbow knuckles blood
brow skin eyes lips bruised

i'm always tougher in dreams
excess muscles mind skill luck
lately they've all failed me
finished in first rounds

when i wake early i feel beaten
sore back arms legs wrists hips
standing naked in a kitchen
waiting on coffee to brew
black donut shop 12 ounce cup

sip swallow sip again
recall fragments of dream fights
i never fully remember them all
it's probably for the best

looking out the window
i tell the fading moon it's irritating
you're a whisky bottle
& it has now been two months
since i last put my hands on your curves

Kiss & Tell

reggie tells a story about a girl
he knew for two weeks
at a petco
says they got real close
one night she stuck her tongue deep into his mouth
swirled it softly
& his legs got weak

i tell him about thursday night at the villa
how my lips against yours
made my body feel like a sun rising
above a city
your exhale becoming my inhale
warmth expanded & alive again

he says bullshit
says he doesn't believe that
i had actually kissed you

& that's okay

i tell him that
i don't believe his story either

That Taste on the Tip of Our Tongues

a cooking show said salmon croquettes
reggie asked
what the hell are salmon croquettes
my childhood dinnertime memory
i replied   i hated them
would sit in defiance until given options
eat it   go hungry
would choose go hungry
& slip out the back door on 7th street
a vacant lot had plenty of red clover
i would chew & suck the sweetness
out of the flowers
thinking to myself
fuck salmon croquettes
fuck options
i was winning the battle until winter
then i thought to myself
fuck winter
i was hungry

reggie said when he was young
he ate a cockroach
on a dare from his father
said it was one of the last times
he ever saw him alive

the mood turned melancholy

i switched the channel to californication

charlie was eating out a girl
that was a squirter
reggie said   yes sir

& i could see in his smile
that he had memories of ex-girlfriends
flooding his mind now too

they were all falling quick & hard

like rain

coming down sideways

Hot Action & Appreciation

you never know if they've a heart
like cotton candy or an accelerant waiting
in a molly bottle with the wick lit

he says   yeah yeah
then tells me he has been thinking
about reciting love words to the next one
that lights a fire inside of him

asks what i think about this

. . . one raindrop drips & splits into two
two drops now drip from moistened lips
so make requests   your hips   your chest
where should this wet passion be placed . . .

that's a good question   i tell him
i've got one that's constantly on my mind

. . . how to make time stand still
truth is i really don't have
the definitive answer for the world
all i have is the nights
sleeping beside you on that couch . . .

he listens   says he likes it
might steal it
whisper it into a woman's ear

& my only hope for him is that
she whispers back

What Am I Going To Do With My Life

reggie suggests i write a graphic novel
real smutty with black & white drawings

he can't read a single word though
i can't draw either   a horrible idea

he says the opening chapter should
be about that one month back in 2008
when he banged several different ladies

isn't that something   he banged several
in one month during a stretch when i hadn't
gotten a single piece of action in almost three

that sounds like a terrible opening

you're just jealous
because i was riding the lightning shotgun
like shooting stars with sunglow albinos
pretending they were all jennifer aniston
while you sat at the kitchen table
exhaling desperation like it was marlboro smoke
from your lips   he says   & your wife
was just as miserable as you

some days   he's a real fucking prick

& i ask myself

how can you argue with the truth though

Nuclear Goodbyes

it's all in your tone
but that's not how you argue anymore
my children tell me
emotions in the waves of voices
have been lost in the leaps
& the bounds of convenience
it's all uppercase letters on a screen now
followed by exclamation points
to make the point
attach an emoji that is crying one tear
angry face
shades of all your frustration
attach another one crying two tears
followed by blue hearts
then red ones
that are broken in two pieces
i shake my head
because what they say is truth
i too have spoken from the gut
without saying a word
i ask my children
how their children's children
will argue with the ones they love
when those rough days
in their futures start to arrive
& they have no clue
i have no clue
guess time will tell
if they will even be given
the opportunity to quarrel

because today
there are still men building bombs
to drop from the sky
on human beings

& that is sadder
than anything i've just said

Traveler

for annie menebroker

you said you had an inconsistent fear
of being lost
yet you knew that one road leads there

compass needles point towards magnetic love

please borrow a burning star from the sky
to hang like a wreath from your front door
when you see our silhouettes

because   annie

we're all coming down that one road now
to visit you

Time Travel

for crissy staton

a bottle of strawberry hill on a saturday night is a magic
potion to make you feel fourteen again

& to remind you that sometimes the wetness of a soul
still needs nostalgic moments dripped upon its tongue

before the choir of reality
sings the moon to sleep once again

Amy

lately my memory has been stalled
twiddling thumbs in the summer of '93
the 8th grade was a notch soon to be
carved   & if the luke-n-karie era
of my hometown hadn't started
it soon would

that summer the rivers knew no boundaries
we knew very little summer baseball
it rained daily
my pitching arm got plenty of rest   but
my heart worked overtime
when it came to amy

she was my sister's friend
her older sister once swore that i chew
my bubblegum like snoop dogg chews his
how strange

she had a five-seven-five telephone number
charged at a local rate & that was a good thing
because grandma would have pulled the
plug on the hour-long conversations
after mere minutes
had it not been

the phone was a small wall mount in the kitchen
there were times that my ass & legs
went numb sitting there

talking to her   she was the first girl
that i fell in love with

one time she spent the night with my sister

i slipped into the bedroom late
to see her   we wasted hours into
the early morning kissing
touching each other on the floor
under a blanket as
the rest of the people in the house
slept soundly

that was the only overnight
i ever had with her

but that overnight
in the blinding darkness
was enough to enhance my senses
& to this day i swear to you
she was an angel
whose wings fluttered through ten-thousand
exhaled breaths
between us

When

a star strangled sky rumbles
it brings back memories
of a summer night

twenty-five years ago

when we crawled on the ground
searching for a lost five-dollar bill
by the short casted shine
of a cigarette lighter's flame

"it's gone for sure"   she said

just before I leaned in
& tried to kiss her for the first time
behind a dying forsythia bush
that I was certain could keep the secret

that there was never even
a five-dollar bill
to begin with

East School St.

my bones ached
from day after day blues

saturday afternoon for three hours
sprawled across a bed
sounds of thunder claps
& raindrops pounding against the roof
beat me to sleep
dreaming

waking up
the sun was shining through the window

i laid there & thought about the dream
i was fourteen again with karie
walking the gravel lot behind esery's grocery store
to the yellow house on the corner
where the porch swing swayed in the breeze
of teenage hormones

on any good day
these days
i'd give half my soul to sit there with her again

Dancing to the Beat of the Bird's Song

the childish soul
that still lives inside of me
knows

that we can't get
that marshmallow soft squish
between our toes

from walking in shoes
on these concrete streets

Yes

you only
live
once

be something
worth
burying

Darwin

what we need

is
to
feed

our brains

a midday snack

of old school
memories

& good marijuana

Editing a Poem

for jason baldinger

*
*
*
*
*
*
*
*
*
*

hearts soaked with 39th st. bustle
a table for ten a jazz   po'boys on plates
po'bodies in seats shootin' shit
cut the first ten   cut the last four
make 'em vanish   bermuda triangles on a tongue
tank 7 in veins   & hours later
you pulled the pins out of your words
like they were grenades   as you marched
the soldiers in the seats through the paths
of your heart   where ghosts leave stardust
residue on the brims of whiskey glasses
just for luck
*
*
*
*

Gin & Tonic Poem

for phoebe carter

the hummingbird travels south before sunrise

her empty glasses on the table
are
    ghosts
            that walk through translucent reveries

In the Backseat

mid-block

we make love
in t-shirts
we make love
with naked hips

traffic never stops

car tires outside roll over (hypnotic)
each revolution makes rumbles
hums in sync
with her
pleasured breaths

& my only fear is that
this moment becomes an isolated event
we only talk about
in private conversations amongst
ourselves

i tell her   "goddamn   baby i'm gonna cum now"

i squeeze her hips hard
with hope

i sweep her hair back
from in front of her golden eyes

Virgin Spring

bumblebees   on trial
stung on a saturday night
fence rows go for miles

god's empty chamber
we live in confinement
    electrical beats

prick between my legs
spinning on a crooked path
lift your dress up high

the songbirds sing
your name in arousing chirps

the young plum trees blush

Sybil

like the clock's
hands

the
bullet moves
slowly

& whistles
a tune

i can hear

all the way
into my
love-blackened
brain

In the State Farm Parking Lot

late evenings

just before nine o'clock

just before the brown sugar luster of street lamps
which stuck in the soft soil
like torches

just before the low beams & high beams
of middle class teens in first bought buicks
blinded passersby eyes
on the boulevards

we walked the streets like royalty

Class of '98

pieces of a puzzle
fit with force & scissors

iris fields at dusk
hankering for time

a delayed operation
an irritation

pearls dangle from gold
skin turns blue like cotton slacks

the moon has fractured

swept away by pride
on the streets of our hometown
we are all glass slivers

A Bookmark for Everette Maddox

sunday afternoon   a river rises
it slips the banks

the buried bones of old possums
float closer to heaven

i pick a poppy petal
& crush it between the pages

its color bleeds onto the
paper   its soul is no different
than yours   or mine

Movie Night

in 1998   harry stamper saved the world
when he detonated a thermonuclear
bomb on an asteroid   i witnessed his
demise unfold from my couch with a
boner   because his daughter grace
really tripped my trigger back then
i closed my eyes with a firm grip &
waited for the explosion

Pam

was my social studies teacher
i was fifteen
she had a smile that made
eight o'clock in the morning
seem very desirable
i spent most classes hugged
up close to the desk with a
hard-on tucked away
like a hand grenade
daydreaming that pam & i
were grinding bare hips in
the utility closet
disregarding age & legal
consequences while d'angelo
sang us to release from the
one small speaker in my
portable disc player

& no matter how screwed up
those days of my youth were
when the bell signified the end
of her class   my soul splintered
like small pieces of butterscotch
that would stick in the rotten
teeth of my awkward teenage
reality

i still wish that we had acted
out & inspired a movie for the
lifetime channel
that ended happily ever after

Taboo

going & coming
streetlights are urban moonbeams
peering in windows

life cycles away
discharged blood on a thrust sword
period passion

soaring with red legs
lust is a floating balloon
dodging ceiling fans

Dammit

i'm right
here

about half a
second away

from
grabbing your
throat

& kissing you

S. Glenwood Ave

for jacob & abigail johanson

even with 4 deuces
& 100 rabbit feet

luck takes a backseat
in a boat shipwrecked on the shores
of a honeysuckle patch

as the metal blades
of a pale blue vornado
circulate a genuine love

on the grounds of your own independence

Lauri

inside my chest
was a cage
without a
perch

my heart
got
filthy

from lying
on its
floor

&
throbbing
for you

Wingless

you can pull all the birds from out of the sky
& try to convince them not to fly
but they will fly again   it is all that they know
they were designed for great heights & long
free-falls

humans were designed this way too
except that they were not given the ability to fly
to accomplish these feats   they were simply
just given the ability
to love

I Fear

that one
day

we may all
begin to
bleed
out

while the
paramedics
diagnose
us

as the
generations

who should
have known
better

Stoned

there comes a time
when you
realize
that the rocks lying
on the ground
have more sense
& purpose
than most of the
people stepping
over them

i see it now
but those poor bastards
are a million years
old & have
known this the
whole time

hardened with
silence & begging
for a voice

We Stand Next to a River

i take a drag from my cigarette   slip my shoes
off take another drink of high life & sit the can
down in the sand   take my shirt off   hang it
on a branch   take my pants off & hang them
next to my shirt   my underwear are blue

i watch her strip her clothes off & hang them
near mine   her underwear are pink & black

the sun is white   hot   & beating down on our
pale freckled shoulders

holding hands   we walk down the bank
towards the edge of a small cliff like two kids in
a cheap slasher film

not at all concerned about the tales of catfish
big enough to swallow men   lying naked in
mud & muck   wearing the slimy coats
of a thousand unfulfilled dreams that have been
casted out with lead sinkers for generations

we jump   shouting with excitement
hands thrown above our heads waving
free-falling without a care

& i wish that love these days
could make me feel
that way again

Pricked

these piles of bird shit
on the ground at my feet
are more tolerable than any form
of human drama   & for that reason
i'm fine with being alone   a great grisly
thorn tree that nobody dares to wrap their legs
around in the lonely seasons of their own depressions

Brandy

i wish that wishbones
were actually
more wishes
than bones

Expiration

when you reach that certain moment
the monster grasps you too

& you learn goodbye is a word
hard to mumble

with fingers pressed against your lips

I Certainly Hope

that the wormy roots
of the oak trees
are allies

that they have
a comforting embrace
like you once did

because sadly

your queen bed
of compressed dimensions
is buried

in a dank cemetery

that is far more suited
for my doggish bones

than for the gracefulness
of yours

Selfish Me

i wish that you could have
gone one more round with
the monster

for one more thomas kinkade
puzzle spread about the
table today

& one more kiss on my
cheek with your coffee
breath that i find myself
missing madly

Kathryn

after the monster won
the final bout
      there has been a great deal
      of confusion

the songbirds now know
no difference
      between the open mouths
      of felines

          or the grapevines

as they perch for the sunrise
in the vacant lot
      which used to be your garden
      of paradise

        & plenty

70 Miles from Dudley St.

i gently burn
the end of this cigarette

i think about you
all of those times
that i lit a last cigarette
of the night & said
"i really don't care
if the monster comes for me"

but now   after seeing
the monster in action
something has kicked the cocky
right off of my wet tongue

the most that i say
at the end of the night now
is that   "i miss you"

then i exhale my soul into
the winds

a wounded gambler

In Comparison

i have
never
minded
crying
because
the roses'
petals
have
never
been
bothered
by
raindrops
much like
the skin
on
my
cheeks has
never
been
bothered
by my
tears
it has
always
just
been
dismissed
as under-
standable
happenings

On an Afternoon

that was still somewhat too warm for
sweater weather   you knuckled up &
fought the monster one last time

at the
final bell

you faded
peacefully
like an oil
lamp's light
extinguished
with grace

& that

is one beautiful way to go

100 Love Haikus For You

one day
i might write them

Sierra

a hickey sucked on the skin above
your heart

the only wound ever inflicted
over & over

without pain

Suddenly Tragic

a glass of water
a flame reaching for heaven
bare knuckles   no flesh

on the battlefield
a voice overpowered mine
screaming into pillows

dreams are a weapon
the bones of cowards will break
darkness becomes light

splinter a second
smoke from a burning grapevine
a snake bites a fool

the blood clot slides north
& waiting with open arms
my brain makes its bed

Father

the future   was once
a yo-yo in the pocket
of my youth   i was
in control   saying
prayers   & eating
vitamins   yet
sacrifice became as
common   as paint
peeling off park
benches
        & dreams placed
on a backburner
eventually meltdown
now this town sleeps
in a cold plot next to
boredom's casket but
my children are alive
educated   & know
love   i hope that one
day their eyes see
contentment   in
their reflection   off
of the vessel   that
compresses my ashes

I.

rust tints pale skin
jagged edges tear holes   completely
through the knees of pants
don't climb the fence   junkyard
hubcaps shaped like waning crescent moons
lean against building walls   last quarter
last dime   last nickel   last penny
forty-one cents
i haven't seen flannery in twenty years
it's my own foolish fault   no longer
a teenage boy chasing girls like clock hands
chase the ghost of a second ago
in a black trench coat   & dancing shoes
with dirty soles

It's Not As Bad As It Looks

for greg edmondson's farm bird

with dingy feathers & soiled feet
you scratched impressions on the wire
as the osage moon illuminated the coop   like
streetlights on the glass door of an adoption
agency   roosting with the ghosts of the
hundreds of children you could never nurture
a factory worker punching the time clock until
death punched back   now the blood of well
intentions drips quietly   greg   will you please
give john a hug   rye whiskey is great & there
is never a good time to drink anything cucumber
half a lime for a pillow & a burgundy wine
blanket are nice   yet irrelevant   when cooked
for hours   in the heat of an artist's heart

III.

for nadia wolnisty

i assume that it is hard for people like us to keep
secrets from the coroner when our body is up on
the slab & our blood is no longer imprisoned
death & coffee are only as dark as you wish
them to be   human brains confuse me   a
switchblade penetrates & i'm not sure i even
mind   i once wrote that i felt like a drunk
hummingbird   you once wrote that you felt
like a firefly leaking light   it's 5:06 pm as i sit
here writing this   raindrops fall down the
window pane & two black birds sit on the
power lines outside   clock hands chase the
ghost of a second ago   & with a finger in the
hornets' nest   we are all eventually bound to
have something wet on the laces of our souls

IV.

& it's always sad to see when the spring desires
become trumped by cold winters that linger for
weeks too long   the robins don't sing quite yet
the sunrise is a silent movie less than exciting
you watch your collection of denzel washington
films over & over again   excited   you crochet
afghans for great-grandchildren with pieces of
your soul in the hooks
you talk about how your body was once a
state of the art incubator   young & dialed in
but how now it's just an igloo for guts & organ
cancers   you sigh & you say   "by god
we should already be seeing daffodils in bloom"
i take a sip of my coffee & treasure the moment

V.

she asks me if i still have a war brain
our dirty fingers picking up garbage that two
stray cats had scattered   a black one with a
white face & an orange one with a short tail
she looks so damn mean with red cheeks
& gritted teeth   she asks
do you think that you can kill them
i remember listening to the radio transmissions
working the overnight shift with sybil   i
remember holding onto her when the car bomb
exploded next to the landing zone that morning
in 2005   now twenty minutes late for work
already   i held an empty tuna can
like it was a lover's hand

VI.

recently i had a dream of a river snaking
through my head   the sign said the *blood river*
yet the water was not blood   the water was not
even red   the water was just water
i sat on the banks of the river & watched
it move around half-buried obstructions
i could see the bottom from where i sat
it was shallow & dimly shimmered like the guts
of a wishing well without coins   last quarter
last dime   last nickel   last penny
forty-one cents   i have never been a rich man
just a dreamer punching the time clock
waiting for someone to reshuffle life
& deal the goddamn deck again

VII.

oh a small bird   oh a seashell
oh a small button from my uncle's coat
for a moment collecting invisible objects
putting them inside a handbag
he walked to her   hugged her   kissed her
walked together to a table beside us
she opened her bag   they looked inside
"oh you found such beautiful things"
i remember how he showed great excitement
for a bag of nothing   just to please the one he
loved   one o'clock in the morning   you're
still angry   gone   dust is gray & thick on the
window sill   i pour gin over ice   swallow it
& wait for the day i make things right again

VIII.

four cigarettes left in pack   ten cigarettes
snubbed in tray   six cigarettes smoked
but not by me   some brains yearn   neon
lights   soft glow of a television screen satisfies
mine   creature of the night is still a creature
come day   someone argues it's certain death
receives replies just depression & survivable
shitty shift work   love learns distance
shadows stretch like gum   eggs cook in a
skillet   strong coffee smells better than a sixty
dollar bottle of perfume   three o'clock in the
morning   cleared throat cocked head   four
o'clock in the morning hot shower water runs
down my body like high hope   towards the
drain

trigger etiquette

if i am going
to take a
bullet,
then so be it,
but please
make sure
that the
son-of-a-bitch
is at least
meant
for me.

after a long fight-night

the mid-summer moisture falls freely
from the morning sky like soft-rotten
peach pits—rotten fruit in full form
disgusts me.

the blackbirds that sit on all the stoplights
& street signs wait like whores for
chewy vittles, as the moisture slips
preened feather tips.

& i just walked seventeen minutes to a
brand new liquor store out of curiosity
& rich rumors of cheap prices, but the door
is locked at ten o'clock. w-t-f?

the blackbirds now snicker & whistle that
the drunks wait like whores too—clever
little fucks. i love them. blackbirds.

they sit high on wires,
they freely shit all over this world,
& it's not the idea of freely shitting all over
something that i love them for.

(although i have my moments where all i
see is a three-ring bullseye, right between the
ignorant eyes of the world)

i love them, blackbirds, because they
seduce me with an any given moment
up & go freedom that aches my
responsibility-grounded bones. blackbirds.

& i tell you my honest desire, darling,
throughout this love me one day,
hate me the next day relationship that we
nurture—if blackbirds could open beer bottles,
then i would seriously desire wings.

i would fly away with my alcoholism
& your whispers for me to *go away,*
no come back, please stay forever,

would never enter my skyward ears again.

the guillotine experts

all say that

the act happens so fast that you'd
never feel a thing,

but how the hell
do they know
that,

they all still have
their heads.

last night

crissy & i ate beef-n-bean burritos
with jalapeno cheese smeared on top,
chicken rice tortilla soup on the
side as we sat at the kitchen table
listening to catfish read a poem about
the statue of liberty's ass on fairfax
radio.

when he finished reading, the other
participants were speechless, crissy
was speechless, & i nodded my head
in solidarity, but in the back of my mind
i wondered if i had lit the candle that
sat in the center of the table, would it
have been romantic enough for her to
consider giving me a jerkjob in the shower
with the V05 shampoo.

i've got some real problems

i've got heroes,
& they got problems
too . . .

knowing this
makes me feel a little
bit better.

second hand

to the young woman
wearing the black
& white bandana,

stocking the racks
at plato's closet,

there are definitely
a hundred thousand
men

who would gladly
fuck you.

gillham park girl

you are a
beautiful dove
beginning to
grizzle from
these dirty
streets
surrounded
by ravens.

i fear
that you will
soon
forget
how to fly
back home
altogether.

barn wood desires

when i was a little boy my nose was
large. it was the size of a full grown
man's nose & i hated my aunt's pig
farm. one day while working the shovel,
i found a secret stash of magazines that
were hidden under the dirty, dead-n-
golden grass in the top loft of the barn.

every morning after breakfast i would run
& climb the rotten peg-steps of the ladder
all the way to the top & thumb through the
pages. i had never seen the inside of a
woman's vagina before, & i had no clue that
a picture could do what it did to my body,
but before the end of that summer, i could sit
up in that loft for hours with a hard-on &
never even smell the shit in the air from the
fresh piles on the ground.

one night lightning struck the loft & it
all ended.

james

an old neighbor told me about
the coffee that he had swallowed
on the navy ships back in the 1960's.

it gets cooked twice, he said, twelve
hours before you would swallow it,
& it tasted like mud. it looked like a
handful of liquid dirt that had been
swept up from the deck. your insides
would itch & your guts would rage.

from that point on, i assumed that this
is how my grandfather felt most
mornings, sitting in san diego,

itching & raging as he pulled his white
pants up to his waist.

i could be wrong though,

hell, he might have never even swallowed
the coffee, i'm just assuming that he did.

i don't know, i have never met the guy.

why i preferred bastard friends

i was the type of little squirt who exclusively
enjoyed my own pillow with baseballs on
the case, blankets with tigers creeping
through trees, that worn down mattress that
sunk deep in the middle, & the four walls
that surrounded it all,

so i was out-of-my comfort zone when i
spent the night, for the first time, with him,
but the evening eased along decently as we
ate cheese pizza, watched hulk hogan body
slam andre at mania 3, built a fort with
bedsheets tied to the knobs of his dresser
drawers, & fell asleep before his older
brother came home at curfew & stumbled
across the bedroom floor.

in the morning we woke up early, lifted his
bedroom window which was on the second
floor, spotted a small brown bird, & wasted
it with his slingshot & a red marble; feathers
flew everywhere as we ran quickly down the
stairs to tell the story to anyone, but his
angry father stopped us halfway through the
story & began smacking his hands against
the back of our heads for being what he
called *stupid lil' sonz-uh-bitches* & we
cowered upstairs in the fort until my
mother got there at noon.

whistling, pretty paper

most all of this broken neighborhood
waits for the drop—government checks
into mailboxes.

the mailman gets a good contact high;
he walks around puddles of piss in summer
winds while whistling willie nelson tunes.

one day, he broke his leg, retired, & now
he waits for the drop too.

pissing on sidewalks again

words are my
young mistress
without flesh.

we share minds

we share heart

we share soul

we share agony

we share lack
of consummation

we share
drunken disturbances

we share bars
between us

we share
smiles,

in photos with rotten teeth.

through your eyes

like ice cubes.
through your eyes like marbles.
through your eyes like the knob
on an oil lamp.

give me confessions from anne,
from sylvia.   cold war kids.
give me buk.   give me the beats.
give me the new to me:
selected poems
six sets, 1951-1983:
howard hart

give me the always open door,
the always open hole;
give me the
oh, baby, you're the greatest i have
ever fucked
lie, because i like it....

like suicide notes without signatures,
my early rejection letters:
five2one   third wednesday
perpetual   gargoyle
lotus-eater   brightly press
cactus heart   word riot

give me cheap wine.
give me fat stomachs & smooth

legs.   give me smoky cunt portraits
in #2 lead & remember
i can draw for hours, when you
use your fingers
on yourself,

consider it,

& know there is no elitism in
choosing
to do so,

the same as there is no failure in
choosing not
to do so,

it is just an option,   a suggestion,

& anyways, i just wanted you to know
there were three-dollar scarfs
for sale at the street fair today,

& i bought one for you.

ashes, but okay

never
hesitate
to be the
one who
starts
the fire,
& then
stands
in the
center
of it;
make
this god-
damn
world
rush to
you, &
if nobody
ever
comes then
just
burn
alone,
&
write
poetry
from the
sweet little
smoked-

out spot
behind
your
charcoal
eyes
just like
the rest of
us burnt-
up-beautiful
fuckers
do.

$3.89 plus tax

i sat down on the shithole
in the back of the supermarket, grunted, &
gave it a good run.

my pants dropped down & covered the tops
of my shoes, & through the crack
in the door, i could see three young punks.

aisle boys & grocery bag boys.

one had large holes in the lobes of his ears
& he said, *hurry up, old man, it's my lunch break.*

& i didn't answer him, i just gave another
good run as i held my limp pecker between
my legs, wondering if it would be a good fit
in the punk's earlobe

& one of the other punks, who had zits
(in all stages of growth) on his cheeks said,
jennifer got some good xtc this time from her dealer.

i wiped my ass four times & stood up.

you fucking stink, like my grandpa does,
said one of the kids who had a nose as large as mine.

it was a beautiful goddamn nose & i
winked at him as i walked to the sink to

wash my hands.
i finished & dried them off with paper.

i walked out of the door.

i pulled my phone out of my pocket &
typed this on a notepad app,

then i bought spaghetti for tomorrow—
sardines for today.

the night owl growl with crissy

i will still be writing poetry
at 2 o'clock while she sleeps,
& by 3 o'clock, i will be beside her
in the bed—my body's weight
cutting ruts in the mattress & my
flash bang snores waking her.

she will sit up & contemplate
carrying out my execution,
while repeating the phrase,
shut the fuck up, through clenched
teeth.

my stay of execution will be granted
around 4 o'clock when she finally
falls back to sleep.

her alarms will ring repeatedly at
5 o'clock & she will tell me later in
the day that she slept right through
them, but by 6 o'clock, she will tell me,
that she was up, dressed, & laughing
at the neighbor's cat licking its own
asshole on the hood of that '84 buick
skylark again.

silly girl

you forget that
i know you better
than anyone;

you forget that
between the blowjobs
& the wine
& the weed

i wrote poems
with you

i wrote poems
for you

we wrote the verbs
& nouns
& adjectives
right out of
our souls

until nothing was left

& that feeling of nothing
felt right

that feeling of nothing felt amazing.

congenital pipe dream

a man's cock leaks equally vital ingredients & we
know that within a woman's womb is the new
generation & the possibility of a future that may not
require the need to constantly hope-n-pray
for an existence that contains peace.

in plainfield, Indiana

the pumpkin spice pancakes
at the cracker barrel could
have been cooked directly
off of the fleshy ass of the
hispanic woman in the blue
dress, who stood in line
waiting to be seated too.

i guarantee you, at that very
moment, that the griddles in
the kitchen weren't half as
hot as that thing was.

excellence

(for janne karlsson)

brilliant bastards
like you aren't
born everyday.

you are 5 aces
in a sealed card deck
of 52

& you haven't
drawn a set of
tits yet

that i wouldn't
gladly chew
on

when this mad
fucking
world,

as we
know
it,

explodes.

road 705 haiku

where the fuck are we
hat on head like heisenberg
strange dogs say, *hello*

untouched

bombs
are beautiful,

so are
butterflies,

but the
problem is that

heartless
motherfuckers

just have to
touch them
both.

buttsex in sunbury, ohio

we drove the white four-door sedan
six hundred & twenty-four miles,

through four states & who the fuck
knows how many counties until it was
almost dark.

we collectively decided that we would
keep left at the fork in the road to continue
on exit 5b, following signs for i-71
n/cleveland until we found sunbury, ohio

& that is where we would shack down.

when we arrived in sunbury, i rented a
room at america's best value inn and suites,
then we unloaded the car—across the street
was a bob evans restaurant.

we walked over for fried chicken, eggs over
easy, hash browns, pancakes, mashed
potatoes, & fresh rolls.

after we ate, paid the bill, tipped the
waitress, walked out the front door & back
across the street,

made it inside room 218,
stripped all of our clothes off, pulled down

the bedsheets, climbed up on the mattress,
& rubbed on each other's bare skin, while
moaning without having to worry about
waking the children, i said to crissy,

baby, i'm gonna try to stick it in the
backdoor real gently, like i did the last time
we made hotel love, six years ago.

she said, *um, no you're not.*

& the feeling of nostalgia hung itself from
the rod, next to the shower curtain.

chicken hungry

the lightness
in my beard
at all lengths
is the same color
as this freshly fried
piece of perfection.

porno daydreams

when my mind
goes obscene & unzips,
i just let it do what it does,

life seems a little more pleasurable that way.

do you remember

when we were beautiful disasters,
when painted black fingernails could have
been mine or could have been yours?

the bullet.   the butterfly wings.

when the weight of the world weighed no
more than the weight of jesus,

my boa constrictor,

a death machine coiled like silk around our
necks & when he would get nervous, our
skin would turn a tender rose color from the
pressure,

& we would laugh,

because we knew that there was always that
funny feeling right before jesus
dropped us to our knees
on the tennis court,

& we were too alive in the moment
to know   that we were actually dying.

meth mistress: poem #1

self-medication & isolation seem to be
the only course of action to beat back
my stalking demon which purposely
wears clothing short enough & sheer
enough that i can see more than just the
outline of her bare vagina when i pass
her in the hallway. *go away,* i tell her,
i already have a girlfriend. she just
growls & licks her lips. yesterday, i
contemplated nailing the windows shut.

meth mistress: poem #2

i often wonder what it would
feel like to be chewed up &
swallowed by a demon with
a mouth as amazing as hers.
some nights i lie on the floor,
less intoxicated than other nights,
with both legs under the bed,
both arms stretched above my head,
just hoping to know & never
have to wonder again.

meth mistress: poem #3

there was one time in a hotel
bathroom, after sex, that she
turned the water on & stepped
into the shower. i sat down on
the toilet & took a shit. you
would have thought that we had
been married for years.

meth mistress: poem #4

i still don't love you,
but i like you enough
to wait for the feeling(s)
to change.

meth mistress: poem #5

& after our fights, i would kiss her throat
& whisper, *fuck-fuck-fuck*
just wishing that my four-letter words
were as razor sharp as hers were,
& if so, if they were, her
pearl necklaces & infinity scarves
would never fit quite the same again.

meth mistress: poem #6

understand that i still care about you,
i just scream & act stupid so that you
won't have to scream & act stupid alone.

meth mistress: poem #7

she told me that her heart
would always be mine,
so i took what was mine
& left him a heartless bitch.

one that now has a reason
to dress in clothes that look
as if she had died last tuesday.

meth mistress: poem #8

she broke me real good too,
my heart now mumbles
obscenities like, *cunt*
underneath its breath &
between its broken beats.
& i let it, because she was
the one who once told me,
your heart knows best.

the day before my 35th birthday

& the red sea inside of me is bottled in
modesto; it rolls over each morning as the
bottoms of my feet hit the stained cut pile.

god is catching a catnap under the couch
cushions. i peel bananas for three-year-old
children & try to shake her awake.

my lips are substitutes for fingertips in all
of my dreams. the first pot of coffee is
never strong enough; the second pot of
coffee is always stronger, but i'm bored with
coffee by that point. i drink beer.

there is a jewel inside the stomach of my
desire.

wake up, god, they are gonna riot in
ferguson soon, but i'm sure you already
knew that, right?

& a machine gun in my sister's hands may
be my ultimate demise, but things can only
get better from here, i'm never certain
though, just human, & intrigued by the possibilities.

& i always assume

that this world
is keeping secrets
from
me too,

but it doesn't concern
me much.

we have never
been all that close anyway.

short stuff: the freedom of my penis

1. on my right hip

these 3 funny moles
the same color as toad lips
grow somber gray hairs

2. on the couch cushions

bowl of fresh salsa
ate early & passed out late
to bat-shit wild dreams

3. s.w.a.t.

my penis captured
in a dream the police seized
this town's most wanted

4. search party

my penis escaped
broke free in a goddamn rush
left a note: goodbye

5. upon return

my escaped penis
came back home three days later
smells like rosemary

6. a question

i can't answer that
is my penis amazing
i'll ask her

7. in her opinion

at times it's little
pastel purple night crawler
at times it is huge

8. & in my opinion

her words amaze me
imma swallow her one day
lips first: safe keeping

the problem

i have suicide bones (remarkable)
see-through & protruding like the
hypocotyl, broken apart & twisted
tight like white bread ties.

these bones have life & thrash about.
they are tough motherfuckers & any
man who knowingly has suicide bones
like mine will understand just how tough
they are.

you can't hide them with the other
skeletons inside of coat closets, or inside
of the cupboards with teacups like all
the other men who love life do.
you gotta have a plan:

plan "a"

hide all my suicide bones in all of these
wine bottles & in all of these average
words.

if plan "a" fails, plan "b"

leave a note—
           gone to see grandma, & bukowski.

i stay naked with

the blankets covering the windows —

it's dark at noon, it's dark at night,
& it's dark as the sun rises.

i control the whole
goddamn environment inside,
& it gives me the time to:

sleep, to clip my fingernails,
to masturbate, to hope, to dream, to write,
to stare at myself in the mirror,
to scribble pictures on the paper that i fail
to write words on,
to smoke, to read, to drink myself stupid,
to drink myself satisfied

& find that feeling that tells me i am ready
to face this fucked up world again.

. . . . now,
the bosses at my job,
they just call it all another unscheduled absence
on my performance record, but i,
i call it,

motherfucking essential to my survival.

porcelain poem

i don't wake with hot breath
& hard bones like i once did.

i don't wake with women &
watermelon seeds stuck to my
skin anymore either.

i just wake soft & clean now,
but i still end up alone in a
bathtub at times,

rubbing myself in ways that
older age & responsibility will
never be able to diminish.

sometimes i never even turn the
water on, i just climb in & lie
flat on my back with the porcelain
chill against my skin,

& imagine your face.

darkness & solitude

kick me in the teeth,
until my choppers
crumble into dust

& i spit them out
like spilled sugar
onto the nightstand,

just to say, *hello*

to the morning sun-
shine peering through
my windows with

bittersweet
greetings & groans.

please know
(for s.a. griffin)

anything that you describe to me as,
rare as pigeon tits wrapped in frog fur,
has my attention.

half dead & half alive

i feel like
an aged man
in this body that
is only
halfway
that.

i sit
alone
for hours
pushing a
pencil.

i don't
speak any
other
languages.

i don't
make good
money.

my neighbors
speak
all different
languages
& make good
money.

they have
scented candles
on their
toilet's
tank.

their
shit
doesn't
smell.

my eyes are
failing me
& my
whiskers
are turning
white.

my guts are
drying out
& my
toenails
are
growing
in.

i have:
acne cream,
hemorrhoid pads,
mouthwash,
& an ashtray
sitting on

the toilet's
tank.

the ashtray
overflows
into the
wastebasket.

maybe one day
i will
put
candles
up there,

but for
now my
shit smells.

it's like a
motivational poster:

PERSEVERANCE.

you on top, top of me

just stay focused, crissy, & keep
pressing on,   keep pressing &
pushing & rubbing against me.

the finish line is rewarding
& we are one slip of your
tongue into my mouth
away from one-hot-mess

& afterwards   as we stand
naked in the bathroom,
rubbing hot watered
washcloths up-n-down our
legs,

you can tell me about how
you almost gave up & i will
tell you about how i would have
never allowed you to

& then we can drink hot tea
in bed, completely satisfied,
until the children wake up
& we once again argue
about whose turn it is this time
to tuck them back in.

my words

have never given
me great fortune,
or fame,

but they have
given me

my sanity.

& i feel that is a fair
trade these days.

when you raise

children,

you
learn
that
the
couch

is a
hungry
monster

that
swallows
everything.

after a little bit you learn

the mornings
come fast
after
closing
the eyes.

it helps
to jump
up right
before you
close 'em,

rub yourself
clean with
hot water,
cold water
& dry rags.

you smoke
cigarettes &
watch 2 a.m.
television,
call the job to
tell them it's
the shits—

bad pasta from
the italian joint
over on
cleveland street,

pour a shot
of gin & a
glass of port,

be a gentleman
& let her
talk about
whatever,
while you sit
undressed
with your
balls
touching
the sofa.

it happens
that way
every now
& again;

it satisfies her,

& then we sleep.

i'm writing

all of our
love scenes
in the
beginning,

because
gunshots
make better
movie plots

& i fully
expect
the closing
credits

to scroll
across a
photograph

of a
tombstone
that reads:

some holes
are opened
with intentions
of never being
closed.

I.

merry-go-round
spinning circles
near the entrance of the
trailer court
barefooted
smashed a honey bee
my foot fell heavy it
plunged its stinger deep
into the skin
damn near to the bone
or so it felt
tender
touched
by older fingers

II.

my foot
bee stung a few hours
before we went to uncle
Rick's funeral
he had suffered a gunshot
i remember seeing my
aunts crying
the stinger inside of
them is one that
will never be removed

III.

sunshine lost
for a split second
you felt like a ghost
punching at depression
with confusion & desire
your red knuckles
wiped on paper swans
looks like a bullet
hit the breast
they lie still in an empty
garbage can like a city lake
in the rainstorm
we touch hands
cross the street
into the sunshine
we find
again

IV.

fallen leaves rustle
two earthworms
underneath
stuck together &
secreting

a peaceful
Saturday morning

V.

this world has gone mad
place a bet for me:
ten grand
that change
is not change

VI.

for heather minette

lonely hearts
mimic stars bursting
into a million pieces
staring at dark ceilings
like two am skies
over Dallas
chests build
pressure
anew

VII.

the birds sing
in trees

mimic sounds of
orgasms

we taught
they learned

VIII.

5 th grade   i took
a deer's heart to school
a gallon zipper bag   girls winced
groaned
i felt like a creep
years later after seeing how cruel girls
had the potential of being
i didn't feel   as bad

IX.

i stand
middle of the road
a dozen coyotes howl
the sound closer
sucking cigarettes
3:27 am
more howls
i'm slightly frightened
too
drunk
to
run
i sit down & laugh
how pathetic i've become

X.

for john dorsey

chicken
chicken fried chicken
food of saints
sinners enjoy too
why all this religious
bullshit in the world
when we could all
just eat breakfast in peace

XI.

dentist's chair   four pm
needle pricks my mouth
in my head it's
Bukowski's *Bluebird*
until the pain stops
the assistant asks
you doing alright?
i let it out
but i don't weep   *do you?*

she has no clue what it's about
& i'm okay with that

XII.

weed with Mandy
a dirt road bridge
skipping English class
kissing under a hot sun

in a wicked garden
dreaming of
responsibilities

that we would now
gladly give away

XIII.

younger
less life beaten
dreaming
trying to catch black birds
from the yard
hide behind a fence on your knees
holding bread in your hand
inching closer to bust again
you wouldn't even know
what to do with it
if you caught it
your mom said each time
you left the sack untied
by the time we were 12
the days of those hunts were over
girls our age started to blossom
the birds went unnoticed
thank goodness for puberty
these loaves last me twice as long now
your mom said
smearing butter on a slice

XIV.

high moon
full frontal

speed bump on the
highway

a snapping turtle's
fractured soul

a vultures fat gut

XV.

front step
sucking on cigarettes
watching a raindrop
kiss Becky's cheek
she exhales smoke
small talk
we walk the slanted
hallway to the bathroom
back inside

XVI.

no paper money
liquor store counter
four-hundred dollars
in a plastic card   but
a broken card reader
means i'm no richer
than the black cat
sleeping on the shelf
behind flavored vodkas
i'm sorry   so sorry
the cashier repeats

XVII.

this morning
jacked off
for lunch
vienna sausages
this afternoon
wrote a good poem
this evening
writing this one
tomorrow
might go to work
then again   might not

XVIII.

first day of June
wine flies wriggle
through open screen
an empty bottle of red
on the nightstand
i've a naked woman
beside me
under thin sheets
we're all just working
for a happy ending

XIX.

Peggy shaved her pussy
left the tail full so
it still felt like a cat
breast cancer killed her
a couple years later
a man with one leg
moved into the house
hung himself one night
in the garage after doing
the grocery shopping
he didn't own a cat

XX.

90 x-strength tylenol
whiskey-n-soda mix
on the bathroom floor
going to die   my soul
going to dance/laugh
i woke late in the day to
start the year 2002 with regret
& gut pains
you think it was
something you ate?
Heather asked

XXI.

a slow roll & stop
dandelions in tarred gravel
preciously postured blooms picked
& rubbed around
my wrist like i once did
as a child
golden bracelet
for hitchhiking blues
cell phones are handy
if you actually have
someone worth calling

XXII.

if i was going to quit
would have done it
when failure felt like
something other than
familiar   first time
successes are not
starting revolutions
finding true loves
she tells you otherwise
be wary
her sugary lies & eyes
melt in vain

XXIII.

for jake st. john

the
moon over my city
soft beams like guy-wires
nailed to a fading horizon
we navigate worn asphalt
dancing footprints in the dust
an obvious trail of our existence
morning time tracks us down
like a hound
with envious eyes
we dream with our heart
about dancing that perfect dance
called
love

XXIV.

blue plastic radiated like
sapphires scattered
across the dashboard
steamed over   sticky
fervid words whispered
an April morning
before separation
his prick in the palm of her hand
as cars drove
down foggy highways

XXV.

inside
like a
thief

burning
the jeweled
box

sparks ran
down my
thighs

XXVI.

wind chimes
the shapes of spoons
tinkle deep soul songs
what the hell we know
about innocence
in a town where sin
is a thin film
layer of dust on a dream
marching towards the
fire   dirty hands swing
near hot hips
flirting with home

XXVII.

moon absconds in a snap
three fingers
swallow from a flask
burn a cigarette
rain falls outside
the phone   silent object
has been for hours
truth is   will eventually
hear from her
she gets lonely
on dark nights

XXVIII.

nobody but bugs
eat here anymore
strawberry beds
grow full of wild
onions
in a tool shed
a rusty hoe
leans against
pegboard

XXIX.

midnight
driving down hwy 65
at 55 mph
fireflies hit the windshield
& die

```
    b       s
      e         h
    a               t
  u                   a
    t               e
      i         d
        f     l
          u
```

i smile
the glass
golden like lover's eyes
shining in
each hello
we speak
through kisses

XXX.

californication
compulsion
out of clothes
free-falling like an arrow
perched on a cloud bed
insides vibrate to release
our cinnamon teeth
find flesh again
on chi-town avenue
gummy bears stick
to the strings of our desires

two wrongs   no rights

she is an angel of death
dipped in   domestic issues
disobedience   & delinquency
she is one certifiable dark-hearted woman
with a small smoke charred brain
    & buzzard claws
every few weeks we have these arguments
& i despise her   so now
as i plot my escape
    i understand you will see
this one day   & think hate speech
but then you will think harder
& realize   it's more like a very good
rough draft   of the truth

she spent

the night
drinking
with friends

&
i spent it
drinking
alone

sometimes

it just worked
better that
way

she stood

in front of a mirror
& turned in a circle

she looked at her body
from every angle

& said

"look at me   i really
don't see how you find
other women attractive"

i laughed   & changed
the subject

she sits on a

polished
hardwood
floor

near the
christmas tree

which is
a plastic
one with
lights
that never
burn out

&

my dark
soul
is envious

of that
tree

one saturday night

i gave her fifty bucks to
buy alcohol   & then i
went to smoke weed
with the father of evolution

she went out & bought herself
something nice to wear before
she sucked a friend's cock
for pleasure

in the morning   she cried
while eating a cinnamon
roll

& i threatened to go screw every
woman that she feared
starting   & ending with
brandy

our emotions

are a dark
wilderness

even when we
know
the safest trails

we still get lost
deep inside
at times

as always

it was
too much
midweek

with a lot

of yesterday
afternoon

women

with wings

are not
always
angels

some just
play

the role well

habitual

you stand   laugh at yourself
& then tell everyone   that it
takes skill to fall up a flight
of stairs   everyone laughs
because you claim to have
mastered that skill   i laugh
because i know that your skill
isn't skill   it's just a great
amount of   percocet & zanax
mixed with vodka   that has started
to mess with your coordination

the only skill   that you have
mastered   is telling lies that
people still believe

she knew

that for
her

there was
a tiny
devil

inside every
bottle

consistently
swallowing

she freed
them
all

her bastard soul

& the truth

are things
that

are not
always pretty

i close the door

over &
over
again

on insanity

but there is no
latch.

i am damned

but i guess
that
there
are
worse

things to be

you have to give

up at times
just to continue

pull the pillow
over your
head

suck your lungs
full

& scream hard
without making
a sound

my throat bleeds
daily

many nights

i rushed home from work
to try & have sex with her
before she got so damn high
that she turned into a zombie

most of those nights   i wasn't
quick enough & i bet that i have
made love to a thousand gym socks
in her absence

some days

ended with breathtaking
beauty

some days ended
with me searching
the top drawers in the
dark kitchen for the
perfect blade to end
it all once she fell
asleep.

the cheaper the wine

the more i will
enjoy

on the day

that i drink
to her
memory

if they call back

then tell them
that i have died

try alcohol   or women.

shit
it's up to you

but i would go all in
& mix them together

tell them
it was a good drunk
with a bad
woman

or a bad drunk
with a good
woman

either story should work

the son-of-a-bitches know me
well enough to believe anything

asylum

straightjackets

because we no
longer have to commit
acts of insanity
for them to
consider us crazy

we simply just have to
walk down
the crowded streets
of our own cities

& attempt to talk to strangers

smeared haiku

we are all colors
vodka with ice at midnight
our dreams don't die

because at gunpoint

everything becomes
relevant

hot-drunk-soft-breath

she always had
my attention

& i constantly
begged
her

"ma'am
   take your finger off of
  the trigger & do damage
     to me with only the cold
  steel of your lips"

& she would

& this convinced me
that romance novels
on nightstands

were written about us

blindfolded   stoned
& fingering her

eventually i found
the perfect touch

which created the
moment

that she still brags
about

when we
get intoxicated

on the
good ol' days

the girl in the flannel shirt   we flirt

it was something out of this world
yet still so simpleminded & normal
like blinking   or drinking
"oh   you're smoking the top notch cigarettes now"
she said with a sexy rich tone & a sarcastic smile   eyes
wide   tapping her fingernails against the glass surface
of the showcase to bowie's *I'm Afraid Of Americans*
she stopped tapping   puckered her lips
stepped back & in a slow motion windmill windup she
tossed the pack of smokes my way
she left a plum-hued lip impression
(with a lip ring void) on the cellophane
i caught the pack at chest level
"thank you"   i said to her
placing it into my left breast shirt pocket
i knew
that she would do it all again tomorrow
& the next day
she has left her lip impressions in a great variety
of shades above my heart for damn near a
thousand days now
opening the door & walking out into the street
i stepped on a wet   rolled up newspaper
with yesterday's news smeared all together
in undecipherable words
it squished under my boot & i knew that
i was now 23 hours & 48 minutes away
from my something out of this world
yet still so simpleminded & normal
like blinking   or drinking

1993

during the daytime
he would mimic his mother
giving thanks for all
things no matter
how small
he mastered his smile
in the shiny reflection of
anything he gazed upon &
during the nighttime
he would mimic his
father
shifting weight from
side to side with clenched fist
shaking them at the
demons inside of himself
from behind his closed
bedroom door
he was his teachers' favorite
student
he was his neighbors'
paper boy
he was a fourteen-year-old
boy with a bottle
of gin hidden
underneath his bed
next to his bible
there wasn't dust
covering either one of them

quiet storm

to talk to him   he openly admitted to every damn
deficiency which manifested behind his eyes   there
were times in the daylight that his eyes greatly ached
so he learned to shadow them with ninety-nine cent
masquerade masks in the back alleyways

he wore the masks while kissing   pressing   &
rubbing his smoky hued whiskers against the cheeks
& chins   & lips of his lovers as he pursued to press
the deities daily by encouraging his lovers to drop one
penny into a pint bottle

because there were never any wishing wells in the back
alleys   but there was always his dirty-hot-hope   & he
learned to deliver his dirty-hot-hope better than any
god   or goddess

eventually the pennies never left their pockets
& it didn't change a damn thing   he already had his
lovers convinced he was the greatest   & i didn't love
him   but i envied him   i was a fifteen-year-old boy
back then   i stared daily out of my bedroom window
which overlooked the alley

his lovers were mine when i closed my eyes & moaned
at nighttime   i rubbed my face against my pillow
softly   like a marvelous pair of tits   i worked fantasy
well   i ground my hips against the bed to the rhythm
of an r&b slow jam

the pucker & blow of my lips

bare knees
&
beads
forty-proof
eighty-proof
i have never
found water
in the wetness
of a kiss
or
displeasure
when a skirt
goes skyward
like all
silk-soft-somethings
once they have
been
influenced
by wind gusts

double down
double down
excite me

like a woman who
understands the
real purpose of
her middle fingers

tom farris

has a meat finger
that can make any
rib blush

& a heart

that this world
can learn a few
good things from

snow angel

after thirty-five
years
of
wintertime   i have
gotten
used to "getting used to"
but i still
dread
each day   it's like sleeping
under
bedsheets
next to
a cold-legged woman with
no
desire left
in
her
breath   or her bones

what i remember

. . . the smell of her sex-fiend perfume
. . . the blade hitting the bone
. . . my eyes snapping shut
. . . her damp breath against my ear
. . . she licked the lobe & whispered
"see i told you that you
would never see it coming"

. . . there was a stranger's voice   a man   & he said
"just take his money & let him bleed out   homicide
division will bitch about him tomorrow morning when
they get the call before the alarm clock wakes them
& they don't even have time to choke down their
breakfast"

. . . she laughed & said   "yeah   fuck him   this is the
dark side of love"

. . . then the door slammed & they were gone
i rolled over & lit a cigarette   my eyes were wet
i laughed as i shook my finger at the ceiling & that is all
i remember
  . . . did they find her

"not yet"   the young cop told him   "they're searching
the alleys south of ninth street as we speak"

i sat in a chair across the hallway shaking my head
listening to it all

remembering the first time a woman taught me a lesson
the hard way about trust
it almost drove me into a desire
to start loving men…

i knew i could punch a man in the face
need be

he's 23 & i'm slightly psychotic

deep
down
i have desires
to invite him over for a candlelight dinner
& slap him across his mouth with my hand
i want to tie him to a chair with my scarf
as my teeth sink deep into each silken knot

i'll snug them tight   until he fully understands
the truth about my head
& my heart

my head & my heart are long distance lovers
my head & my heart both pound
my head & my heart are the new age terrorists
my head & my heart spin 'round

& after he hears all about me
i will set him free   & give him the
opportunity to choose

number 1) hand jobs as we listen to the kansas city
symphony   or number 2) make fresh vegetable soup
& biscuits   or lastly number 3) run away

& by morning light   i hope he has chosen them
all in progression

against heads like hickory wood

mornings   i drink my coffee & look out the
car windows
i'm simply a writer riding
but
i
have
come
to the
conclusion
that
too many men's skulls need a reminder of
what
primal means   &
beautiful women
refuse to believe that
they are actually
ugly
when
they cry
the truth is
these city streets are a
self-indulged
stuck-up-the-ass
horror show   & a seven-pound hammer swung wildly
is not a
guaranteed
resolution
but it's a damn solid suggestion

the gods

are serving
from the
slaughter house
floors

the governments

are handing
out spices

will this life
ever taste good
again

junkie paradise

there is a reason why i dislike public restrooms
they always seem to leave me with a not-so-pleasant
story to indulge   but i had to piss   so i took care of
business   & later that evening at dinner   i told crissy
"there was a syringe floating next to a dollar bill"

may thirty fourteen

the sun beats hard   i can see the sweat glisten
on the young lovers' arms   as they sit there taking a beating
christ they are going to stink

they hold hands & squeeze tight at the knuckles
with each free hand pressing cigarettes tight between fingers
& lips   she has lips that i like

he has a cigarette without a filter & horrible lips
i light a cigarette myself & sit in the shade
she just kissed his horrible lips   poor girl

i wonder if they fuck   i have sat here long enough to
already have fucked her a few different ways in my mind
the clouds cover the sun & everything is now shaded

the lovers stand up to leave   i can see the sweat stains all
up her back   she smiles with her lips when they walk by
i smile too

his lips have a sheen of spit on them   but it only gives them
a different look of horrible   i watch them gone & then
take out the couple pieces of paper that are folded up in my
pocket

one is the start of a writing from yesterday   the other one
is blank   i put the blank one back & start writing where i
had left off

the sun is back now   i wish the lovers were too

drying out

forty-six days ago things were alive
& beautiful   fish swam like fish
frogs croaked like frogs do
but forty-six days of drying & dying   & the
fish just don't swim anymore   & the frogs
don't croak quite the same
window-sash-cracked-open-air isn't even
enough to stir about a good finger job
as i suffer with her heavy legs draped over
mine   heat-induced lightning has become
soft foreplay   it's a rough colored golden
flicker somewhere between the skin tone
of a pumpkin   & a thin slice of cheddar
"just get up" i tell her   "i think that
tonight is the night"   & after an hour
of sitting on the dirty front steps
as the lightning dance battled
with sharp points through the clouds
nothing gave   "i'm going inside"   i tell her
"i'm going to sit naked   & fan myself off
with a magazine"
i strip down   & i work a two-month old
redbook the best that i can   & she lies
beside me stretched marvelously
sucking wetness from a glass with a straw
dry   hot   teased   & damned
"i think only the long bearded man who sells
the snow cones on the street corner
loves droughts like this"   i tell her
& she agrees

life changing

they say that
the fires of hell

are hot   but i do
not fear the heat

i fear that hell
will smell like the

scent of your perfume
on my pillow at

two in the morning
as i lie alone desiring

you   trust me   that
misery alone is worth

finding some kind of
god to believe in

when the only woman that really loves you tries
new things in bed just because she wants
to feel like she is continuously pleasing you

let her   a finger in the asshole
may be uncomfortable   but has
never been as uncomfortable
as loneliness

my monster

once again   she
ripped & clawed her way
through the
     tough layers
 of
"i'll never love you again"
    & i let her

i'm a weak man in my nightmares

deb

i used to wake her
late at night
& we would shower
together   washing
each other clean
prior to sitting outside
& smoking small cigarettes
as we gazed the sky
for falling stars

i haven't seen her in
in three years

our son
hasn't seen her either

it came easy for us

some men never survive well with women
some men never survive well with themselves.

years ago   i had a woman who once desired
to drink as much as i would drink
but she could never do it.

she had a fat stomach   light hair on her head
& dark hair growing in the space between
the cheeks of her ass.

she had a soft tongue   a hard heart   & i enjoyed
it all.   we would both wake in the early
afternoons with haggard faces & bones that felt fractured.

we showered together   & both pissed golden
yellow streams onto the shower floor
but i didn't mind her piss   & she didn't mind mine.

we just let loose as the hot water brought us
back to life for a few hours   & not a damn thing
else mattered back then   we were surviving

& it was good enough
that i swear the world could have murdered itself
right outside our window

& we wouldn't have cared enough to even open
the sash & shout out through the screen.

feeding my demons

i hated looking at my ugliness each morning
in the mirror   i was convinced that there were
small demons living inside of me   so i would
drink every day   & then every night i was drunk

i would hold her body down against the bed's
blankets against the living room's carpet   against
the car's front seats   against the hallway's stairs
or against the lamp post that stood outside.

i would squeeze her wrists with a persuasive force
heavy enough to crush plums in my palms
& it would leave filthy-finger marks on her skin.

she was never defiant during these times   & i
would beg for her love with hot sangria breath.

she would tell me with her gentle voice   be kind
don't be an asshole   this world already has plenty
of assholes.

i would let loose of her soon after this
& then we would finally cook dinner

we never ate before midnight.

love letters

i blamed her   because someone had to be
blamed & it didn't matter what she tried to say—
i goddamn swore to her face that she had found
them   & did as any jealous lover would have
done   destroyed them   & denied ever knowing
their existence.

she denied knowing their existence   of course
& when i told her that they were last hidden in
the bottom of a cooking pot   which was in the
bottom of the large box that had some other old
pots & frying pans on the top of it   she laughed.

why are you laughing?   because just the other
day i gave that large box to the lady next door
who was collecting things for the church   she
replied.

what church?   the baptist church around the
corner she said.   i hurried to put on my jacket
& told her i spent years wrapping them in
bundles & hiding them in different places   so
that each new woman couldn't find them   &
you ruined it!   you ruined them!

i rushed out the door before she could say
another word   & once i made it to the church
steps every door was locked.   i walked around
the drive twice before i found the trashcans

hidden behind a picket fence.
i climbed the fence   & in the bottom of the
third can that i tipped over were my old love
letters that i had never sent   but saved.   i sat
down on the gravel & opened one.

it was one that i had written last year to michelle
it was written in all capital letters & the
beginning said:

OF COURSE I'M NOT PERFECT   CHRIST
IS THAT WHAT YOU THOUGHT   THAT I
WAS PERFECT?

i sat there wishing that i had given that letter to
her. i wished that i had given all the letters to all
the women i had written them for   & vowed
that one day   i still may   but on that day   i
just walked back home

& waited for her to leave   so that i could hide
the letters once again   & if she is to find them
then so be it.   i guess she will know my misery.

phallic & forgotten

you have walked away
& left me standing alone
holding what you describe
as the future   in the form of this
dead   white-dickheaded dandelion
pinched with my fingertip grip
& i'm not sure if you understand
that tonight's weather forecast
is predicted to be rough:
high winds & heavy rains.

you have walked away
& left me standing alone
& i am certain that this
white-dickhead in my hand
already knows that i am not a god
or an unbottled genie that can
answer its prayers   or grant its wishes.

you have walked away
& i have looked at this thing from
every single angle   i even turned the
white-dickhead upside down   thinking
that maybe the answers were
hidden up there.

a small voice inside me asks   what will you do?

shit-if-i-know   i can talk to it.

i can ask it questions   & look like
a fool to all the strangers on the street
when they see me engaging & saying
excuse me   i understand that in your
current state   you have an ultimate desire to
recreate & continue existence
to be scattered about & seeded
but how do you want this to happen?

do you wish to be blown away?
do you wish to be beaten off?

& when i receive no reply   then what?

you have walked away
& left me standing alone
& i just want you to know
that i put thought into this decision
& i have now decided that i
am going to simply give it the same advice
that you have given to me
so many times

& then place it down on the sidewalk
& walk away.

—figure it out yourself   dickhead.
i don't have time for this.

a garden plot

when i become
silenced
   seduce me in
my days after death.

plant tiger lilies
& let them
roar above my
head,

sway like stiff lace
in the wind's gust &
stretch up high like
   the fat legs

of a woman towards
the mountaintops
   the blooms will be
labias & beautiful—

let them live there
at least a week
   or two   or three
or forever.

november 10th

i was hungry   but couldn't eat.
i swallowed two more vicodin (pretending that
the first pill was potatoes & that the second pill
was hot brown gravy) they both hit an empty pit
in my stomach as my tongue rubbed against
each tooth that remained   another dry socket
& i sat confused with three socks—two white
socks on my feet & a black sock on my left
hand.   i'm right hand dominate.   i have always
been right hand dominate.

the weather man inside the clock radio said
prepare for a night colder than any night we
have seen yet this year   & can someone please
check on the homeless?   there was a shelter that
closed its doors today.

pocket change   the chiron review issue #97
an old pair of eyeglasses   a stained coffee cup
a stained wine glass   animal crackers   & i
scratched what was left of this pencil with the
only sharp object i could find in all the clutter
that was lying on the nightstand—a pair of
fingernail clippers became dull with lead dust
but i had exposed enough to write with   &
enough was simply all i needed.   i wrote
despite the ache in my head   i wrote slowly   i
wrote

— sometimes you just have to laugh at
responsibility & then slaughter it.   be bold &
do it like i do it . . . choke it with dirty fingers
& then bury it under some broken acorns & oak
leaves near the trees that all the stray dogs piss
on. i know it all sounds crazy & makes no sense
but sometimes it has to happen that way.   you
gotta make it a goddamn horror show & satisfy
yourself. the last time that i slaughtered
responsibility   i sat across the street in my car
with the window down smoking newports until i
saw the stray dogs coming & then i was
satisfied.   i drove home   & washed my dirty
fingers back clean before i dialed her phone
number   she answered   & i told her   baby
i am ready to love you again—

by this point the pencil needed worked over with
the nail clippers   but i didn't have the desire to
work it over.   i had the desire to smoke a
cigarette & even though i knew that my desire to
smoke cigarettes was fully responsible for my
aching predicament   i once again chose to
slaughter responsibility for desire   & as i sat
there inhaling through the misery   the frost
danced designs all over the windows outside &
the voice inside the clock radio said

it's now twenty-nine degrees in the city   & by
request   this next song goes out to amanda
who lives on the east side of kansas city
paul loves you.

writing a bunch

of small
poems about
snow

that suck just
like their
muse.

i'm going to
set them
on fire
in the
ashtray

& write new
poems

about the
piercings
in your
nipples &
navel—

new poems

about
that missing
taste of
metal on
my
tongue.

with her

i
moaned for
minutes

& have
ached for
months.

when we get

stoned

& play
sex games,

i am always
allen ginsberg.

she loves
ginsberg

& lets me
put my
cock in
her asshole.

goddamn,
ginsberg,

thanks man.

i kissed

your forehead
& naked stomach
before i climbed out
of bed this
morning

& i could still smell
the md 20/20 in the
air from your
breath.

you swallowed enough
last night

that you started
to recite poetry,

& i have come to the
conclusion:

you just might be
my soulwhore.

she's unicorn pretty

i'd fill the hole
in her head
with

cotton candy
& love her

until the
insects
finished feasting

&
time
took her
bones away
from me.

sometimes

a fat lip
is the
prize

that
tomorrow
will bring.

just crawling

bare chested
through
wet grass,

in night's darkness,

hoping the
worm's path
brings sense

before the
morning sun
leaves you dry,

& stepped
over

by this city.

you set water on fire

with your fingertips &
act surprised that i say
"you fucking amaze me"

…silly woman
burn me

she is a

filthy snake,
& he is a
filthy rat.
i have no doubt
that she will
try to swallow
him whole
tonight,
starting with
the head of his
dick,
& ending
with just another
bag of
love-bones
that she will
tote around
in her guts
for a day or
two—
just like she
once toted mine.

when i was an older boy

smack-dab in the pubescent
choke hold & accompanying
powerbomb,
growing thin ginger hued hair
on my lip & on my chin,
awkward, walking around
with a body covered in acne
like an active minefield
half detonated with scabbed &
scarred casualties left lying in
the sun, salicylic acid 2%
covering them,
horny, & inexperienced—
i dreamt of a woman sitting
naked, straddling my face like
they do in fuck-films.
Lora, my first, slightly shorter
in height than i was, smack-dab
in the choke hold & powerbomb
herself, had dark hair,
smelt like a cherry field, &
showed me on the day that i lost my
virginity that dreams can come true
when she straddled up on me;
i let my tongue loose with a fury
of punches like a prizefighter,
swinging blindly.

chasing

each other's tongues
in our mouths,
quick movements in
opposite directions,
causing an unstable
atmosphere.
i was radical lightning,
free-falling,
raging with my
teenage chemical
messengers.
i collided with her insides,
creating a forest fire
that burnt carelessly
out of control;
my spunk was the fire
& everything feminine
in her pelvic plot was
orgasmic ash & ooze—
weeks to months later,
as organs & eyes were
created in succession,
a human being emerged
successfully from inside
of her.
& this was the beginning
of my challenge.

she came back

two days later
with a pistol
in her hand
& i figured
that sure,
she probably
deserves at least
one good shot
at me,
but i never
opened the
door to give it
to her.
—hmmm, maybe
i really am the most
selfish asshole she
knows.

at the time

i was a fifteen-year-old boy,
& she was a fifteen-year-old girl
who said to me,
"if you really love me, you will do it."
love at fifteen years old? shit.
i had been convinced that i was
in love with her for a whole year
prior to her challenge.
she offered her tits to me, &
one hand down her pants for the
first time.
i would have probably murdered
my own father that night, or sucked
the itch oil straight out of a poison
oak leaf
if she had asked me to, but she
didn't; she simply just asked me to
smile, & i did.
i showed her how crooked & sad
my lips sat on my face & she loved it.
she let my fingers conduct
an orchestra inside of her,
& i loved it, & i felt it,
& at times i still feel it—
it feels just like the rain sounds
at 2 a.m., passionately pattering all
my window panes,
& i smile. my smile is still crooked,
it's crooked & older, much older,
twenty years older, & i miss her.
somebody please tell her so.

& i'll either

act
like i care,
or i'll fake
like the
spinach salad
has turned
my guts into
soup.
you just might
learn the hard
way, darling,
that i can sit
for hours
alone
on the toilet
smoking
cigarettes
&
writing poetry
all over
the pages
of your
Women's Health
magazines.

most nights

the most
important
thing
is
her
cocktail glass.

all my beautiful

bedmates,
that were as
hot as the
summer's
sun,
were also
eventually as
cold as the
winter's
moon.
most days i
just felt like a
fool,
springing with
excitement
& falling
with
disappointment
while the
dates fell
sharply
off the
calendar.

i don't waste

my days
searching
for beautiful
women anymore.
beautiful women
don't waste their
days searching
for me.
see, in the end,
they were all like
books
filled with a
thousand blank
pages,
& i ruined
every single one
with my words.

yeah

i grew up
too.
i'm working
the same
job
everyday,
& hoping
for the more
exciting
side of
death.

i once saw a

man do a
backflip with a
slight twist
from the
top of a
brick wall,
that was taller
. than i was
tall.
when he
landed
on the ground
with both feet,
he shouted,
"fuck yeah, kid.
i'm the king
of the world.
i'm the only
man that
Death fears."
& i believed
him,
all the way
up until the
day
that he died.

somewhere

at this very
moment,
in this
black-eyed
city,
life is kicking
somebody's
ass
three inches
away from
a last resort
feeling
of the need
to induce
a self-inflicted
ending,
but right here,
i just want
to wake up next
to your hot legs
when the alarm
clock begs
for obedience.

sometimes

it is just
your body
that i need
in the bed
when i
wake,
so please
know
that when
i call you
to come,
it is
because
your
levels of
pleasure
have age to
them &
understand
all my
levels of
loneliness.

& when

you have
finally
figured it out,
you will wake
up sober
& remember
nothing.
it's okay
life is laughing
at us all.

1.

ginger &
grit;
there is art
on my tongue,
come
here
& taste it
with yours

2.

weapons...
the men in the back
alleys have blades &
bullets...

all i have is
a pencil & my mind...

is that dangerous enough for you,
        darling...

4.

whisper soft like tiny raindrops
& i'll lean closer

6.

you beat upon my
heart with both
fists.   you are my
favorite bruise.

9.

you are a skyscraper of desire
            erect in my heart…
my chest bulges
            to near explosion
& it amazes me
            how i ever manage
to button up my shirts these days…

11.

i'm guilty...it's my
caring & compassion that
have created all these damn
crime scenes.

13.

her lips
are a puppet;

her emotions are tiny strings…

& the greatest show
that i have ever watched…

is how they danced
in the darkness
against mine

18.

the women
were
all
songbirds;
i wanted every
goddamn
one

19.

write it.
erase it.
it's your
love story
until
the end.

27.

FYI
i have never been an
            innocent victim…
            & tonight
there is a riot inside
            of your eyes…
    come here.

33.

the wrinkles & scars
on my cheeks fill full
like canyons in the
flashing seasons.

i cried for her yesterday.

i cried for her
today.

35.

before alcoholism, my
toughest
addiction was
my love for the
manic inside of
a depressive
woman.

The Day Before My 36th Birthday

and between bites of a chicken &
cheese quesadilla with black
olives & pickled
peppers,
my four-year-old daughter
says "Asshole".
i keep chewing and ignore her.
"Asshole" she says, tugging my
arm & i nod my head.
she gives one last hard tug at the shoulder &
pulls my head down closer to hers;
my ear is at her lips.
"Poopy Asshole" she says & i swallow.
i pat her on the head with my hand & send her to fetch
her mother.
she leaves the room.
she returns with a warm dishtowel
just recently removed from
the clothes dryer.
i shove the last bite of
the quesadilla shell
through my lips, chew it, swallow it, & wait . . .
"Asshole Poopy Asshole"
i watch her swing the white, but
stained from spilled grape juice
towel from side to side like a marching band's
flag & it twirls fast.
it twirls then falls limp.
"Asshole" she says again & this time

i smack the wooden table top with
both of my hands
like i remember seeing
my own father do so many time before.
my hands make a thud &
i shout
"ENOUGH!"
she shouts something mumbled
& runs from the room crying.
the dishtowel lies alone
on the floor as her mother walks into the
room & says
"do you always have to be such a goddamn Asshole?"
standing behind her is
my daughter who wipes her eyes &
grins while she peeks her head
around her mother's right hip.
i smack the table again for good measure
& pick up my milk glass.
i drink it & sit it down;
the milk runs slowly down
the sides from the brim.
my daughter laughs victorious, prances down
the hallway,
& i walk to the stove for a second
helping of dinner.

Tutoring

"I can't hold back, it's like having a hundred million little heart attacks"

—Prince, from the 1992 single, *Damn U*

"2 Whom It May Concern"
wasn't relevant, it was just a song
on the B-side of the cassette that i played
for her that day in '93, as she

pressed against me on the living room
floor after school. she laid on her back,
& i on my side, one hand under
her shirt for the first time,

exploring the soft purple cotton of the
bra which held her blossoming
teenybop breast.

i whispered to her selected words from
"Damn U" & hoped like hell that my
grandmother would come home late
from work that day.

A Year and a Half Ago in a Hotel Room

it was a mandatory meeting. i needed it.
we were exposed without bed sheets,
bare asses, & the hands of the clock watched it all
as i licked my lips with spit first, but before i
finished, he had done the same to his,
licked them.
we lit a cigarette & i held it between my scarred
fingers while we sucked smoke like foreskin
through lips still dry like burnt breadcrumbs
the spit was worthless.
the room filled with ashes & haze
until the mirror no longer showed my reflection.
i puckered my crusty lips & blew madly
in all directions until the room cleared &
gave view of the mirror once again
my reflection visible once again,
bare asses visible . . . once . . . again.
i cleared my throat, fingered my nose
& wiped my eye
i read the latest book review from
the *Plainsman Press*
& it was nicely written. it complemented my
work, so we came to the decision that there
was still a life for us beyond these walls.
nobody voted for suicide,
so i dropped the cigarette
into a cup of water, adjourned the meeting &
untied the rope from the ceiling rafters...
the golden girls were on the television,
laughing, muted in the background.

We Are Sin, I Suppose

i'm limp & stretched thin at 9 a.m.
drinking coffee that doesn't
have much of a knockout punch
from a 4-dollar cup, & sure,
i understand that a man should
regularly try to shove it all into
the great glory hole of well
intentions, but today isn't
my day . . .
tomorrow, hell, it could be . . .
& i just might shove it straight
into your asshole, & save the small talk
for when we have coffee cups
in hand. two cups will cost us
8 dollars. jesus christ. why do
we still drink here like
hipsters? fucking typewriters.
click. click. click.
& i'm now reading
alicia young:
"the way married people"
& scanning this room for
neck ties.

Keep Moving! Do it Now!

the night sky rains powder
it rains hot gas & brains
short circuit

the media shows it all

god never concocted rain like this
it's man-made rain to be inflicted
on man

. . . . . encroachment

the respiratory command
centers get overtaken
& the elevators that run up
& down the spinal shafts
stop working —

tongues hang out touching
chins until all the muscles
that have never known
confusion
learn confusion

the jaws & eyelids snap shut
clench tightly like rusted
door hinges   &

noses are all that men have left
to gasp from

as canisters clink against the concrete
like ice cubes against the bottom
of my empty wine glass   &

people are all son-of-a-bitches
choking on both sides of
what is right & what is wrong

i am two hundred & six miles
away from the rain that falls
in Ferguson   & i am
a son-of-a-bitch too . . . . .

don't shoot   sir

i am only reaching
for the television remote

Broadway Street

buttercup yellow boots with this
toad-belly-tinted dress
is the perfect mix of hideous
& she doesn't give a damn
what she looks like at one
o'clock in the morning, or one
o'clock in the afternoon.

she walks beside me & i
don't give a damn what she
looks like either.

"should we stick-up the corner
store & rob 'em blind, baby?"
she asks & i remind her that
she is the only silly twat
wearing buttercup yellow
boots.

she laughs & calls me a pussy
in black plastic glasses; i roll
my eyes & open the door.

the corner store smells like
corndogs, & she hates that smell,
oh well.

i can eat a half dozen with
ketchup, but no mustard & i ask her,

"baby, do you remember when the
Blockbuster video store used to sit
next to Chubby's Diner?

Love

is a wildflower
growing mad

all over the hillsides
of every man's soul.

Sorrow

"have you ever wanted to kill yourself, kill yourself
because of a girl?"

"sure, i have considered suicide before. hell, homicides
before too. at my age a man has been around long
enough to have seen, or read several instances of both.
it in a way gives a man many options, so many options
that he becomes indecisive, unless of course, he is just
impulsively crazy in his head, or crazy in his heart."

Absinthe O' Blue

the sky is a glum color
of battered reality.

dreams, oh beautiful dreams
turn to nightmares,

as the prostitute puts on her shoes
& returns to the streets
you could never pave in gold
for her.

Turpentine

you need no ears to hear what is
being spoken inside your own head,

something isn't right though,
the straight lines are stale & fatty

sticks & stems must have bends
to dance in the hospital garden,

bristles & lips are now soaked,
& dr. rey looks on from a distance

knowing that there is pure brilliance
within the man who wears the bloody
bandages.

Mental Murder

a woman once swore
that she would walk through walls for me
but she never did
she only used the front door & the back door
until eventually
even those were too much to maneuver

i honestly never even locked them
most nights i left them ajar
hoping she would sneak in
close them before some madman crept in
from off the street & murdered me

but i woke in the mornings alone

i eventually just assumed
she had fallen in love with the madman
& that my slow death from loneliness
was a joint effort

Dancing with Rosalea

the stars in your sky
are ignited by burning pitchforks
lifted by angry men's hands

i want to tell you
to put on a black dress & find shoes that match

if scuffed no problem

we'll spit
on the harper county dust
& polish it away with a rag until they shine

i want to take you out dancing
rosalea

to a place where the jazz
takes you back to the days
when you were a younger woman
in nyc

to a place where you can exhale without
hate's pressure on your chest

to a place where you can say
tonight
i could die in peace

because i fear

you may never know how that feeling feels

Public Enemy

if she had a clock
hanging from her neck

rosalea would turn back time

to better days

when the moon
was something lovers
gazed at

from a hotel window

long before the flavor
of the phrase
            fight the power

crossed the cracked
thin skin
of her aging lips

Space Camp

i never went to space camp
but one summer
reggie said his drunk mother
had packed his bags
the night before he left
as she expressed all her concerns
so in the morning as he hopped on a bus
with three rolls of toilet paper
& twenty-seven yards of aluminum foil
in his backpack so that he
could keep his asshole clean
& build a fancy hat
that would shield his brain
from unknown creatures
i laughed hard at him
& he swore
that back then
traveling through six states
was still not far enough away
from his miserable life

I'm a Writer, not a Fighter

& on the nights when
my busted lips
   tint the ice cubes red,

& she sits there for an hour
letting the melted water
     run down
her soft cold fingers,

i tell her,
  "even superheroes take a few
  good punches, darling
nobody can dodge them all."

she always laughs kindly,
then reminds me,
"sweetheart, i have yet to see
     you dodge one."

The Neighbors Never Sleep as well as They Once Did, but They Still Sleep

her lips
extinguish
me when
she grabs
my shirt
& spins
me around.

i exhale,

but when
she ignores me,
i just stand
there
against
two walls
with my face
pressed tight
into the
corner
& let out
screams
with my
bones on fire.

there are
nights that i
burn
to death.

With Sharper Teeth than We

a pack
of wild
dogs
can chew
your guts
out,

but so can love.

the human
body is
a feast.

A Healthy Misery

my prostate
is
healthy
& my
pecker
still
stands up.

it's impressive,

but that
means
nothing
when your
kiss
is no
longer
desired.

A Monarch, I Was

her touch was
beautiful.

i was beautiful.

i was,

but now,

i am a common butterfly
flapping my
fingerprinted wings.

i am breathless.

i am perching
on street corners
now.

i am watching
mass confusion.

i am at the mercy
of the wind.

i gasp with
dissatisfaction,

& catch hot love
on the cool side
these days.

Susan

a soul tasted,
teased, not taken.

a million men
float unspoken,

but the one whisper
in the crowd
was precarious.

her eyes
were twined,
black licorice
& lipstick.

a mass burial
of minds fucking,

& she was
content to walk
all over the graves.

I'm Down to the Days & Nights

hope is like
a mistress—

something to
hold onto
when what a
man knows
becomes
normal,

&

once all the
mistress moments
become predictable
& hope becomes
over-thought,

it is then

that a man
can live
his life
with only
what is
before him—

his days &
nights
of salvaging
reality.

Before the Ending

with my right hand
underneath the nightshirt
of morning time, i held
her breast tightly.
it was
the only time that sober
seemed survivable.

Masturbating To Her Picture

she smiled
& was
holding
her phone.

i was drunk.

i closed my
eyes & woke
in the morning
unfinished.

i rolled over
& picked the
picture up.

i walked to
the icebox
& grabbed
the last
bottle;
it was empty
& she never
stopped smiling.

i was sober
& defeated
again.

If I am Lucky I Will Remember Them

a pain pill,
a soldier,
a nurse,
have all
hardened me
in days
before.

today i lay
naked with
nine o'clock
darkness
surrounding
me.

my balls
in my hand.

i am limp.

the rain beats
madly against my
windows
like
drunken lovers
from my past.

i dream like a man,
tossing & turning
the sheets off
of the mattress.

It Triggers This Memory

i remember being
16 years old &
standing in a room
watching the residue
of cancer being sucked out
of her stomach through
tubes.

"you may not recognize her,"
the doctors & nurses said,

& they were in a sense
right, but i remember the
tubes because they were
black like summer asphalt.

i stood there for
thirty minutes just watching it drip
slowly while not more than
five words were said.

i tried to talk, but

death has a way of making all
things speechless.

Lips

responsibility
is a
porcelain
platter,
& we
have
shattered
it a
million
times with
drunken
lips.

Beating Winter Moments with Summer Memories

i remember
standing
in a
crowded
market,
& the
people
surrounding
me
were
ugly.

the
children
were
ugly.

they were
standing
in lines
with their
parents.

the men
were
ugly.

the women
were
ugly.
i was
standing
in line
with my
parents,
& we
were
ugly too.

it was
a cold
morning
&
everyone
was
dressed
for the weather:
long pants,
long sleeves,
hats,
scarves,
gloves.

it was a
hopeless
gathering
of disgust.

i took
my gloves
off to pluck
a petal loose
from the
fresh roses
that were
wrapped
in plastic
at the end
of aisle 3.

that petal
was
nothing
like
the crowd.

i rubbed it
between my
fingers
& it was soft.

it
reminded
me of
beautiful
things,

like warm
cotton candy,
or the

babysitter's
legs
under the
covers
when
i
was
seven.

The Moments That Stay in The Back
   of a Mind

the plants suffer
until they
are near death
& the leaves
cower towards
the floorboards.

come payday we all drink.

the plants spring
back to typical
erect posture
& we all
feel satisfied.

we are content.

we listen to,
Audio Content
& i tell them
of the days when
derek & i
would wake early
& fish together
from his father's
small boat.

we were small boys
& the days were
summertime.
they were simple &
they held moments
that would make up
conversations
on friday nights
many years later.

have you ever seen
a plant smile?

show it death &
then drown it back
to life.

tell it stories of
a beautiful man
& then promise to
do it again—

it works every time
& we sober up
together.

I Remember

on the side of the cheek:
my grandmother's
peppermint kisses

on the top of the head:
my grandfather's
whiskey hands.

A Night without a Muse

i'm hungry,
but not real hungry,
i'm putting out a
cigarette,
i'm drinking beer,
i'm drinking wine,
i'm listening to
the ignorance of
hollywood,
i'm listening to
children cry,
i'm watching car
doors slam,
i'm rubbing my
tongue against a
broken tooth,
i'm trying to rub
the tooth against
my tongue,
it is my play on
words with friends,
my skin is dry from
the weather,
the dogs are
barking,
i'm sitting with a
pair of broken
eyeglasses hugging
the bridge of my

nose & one ear,
i'm lighting another
cigarette,
there is a pan of
burritos on the stove,
there is a naked woman
in the shower,
it's 6 degrees outside,
it's 70 degrees inside,
it's 70 miles to my job,
it's 6 blocks to the
liquor store,
my house slippers are black,
my socks are not on,
i'm pouring another drink,
i'm scratching my stomach,
i'm scratching my neck,
i'm scratching my head
& still don't have shit to
write about.

Eating Religion

stomachs,
hearts,
heads
& souls

all
swollen
&
bloated up
like
wet rice

it all
produces
shit,

day after day.

They are all Simple & Look Alike, but I
   Paint Them Anyway

love is no longer
oil based &
life is no longer
stretched canvas.

at the very
best
these days,

it's watercolors
on napkins.

i feel like a
little boy
again.

i am still
alive.

i am still
dreaming,

& i am
painting
blue birds
for the
icebox.

Broken Bottles & Bus Fare

love is a mass transit
swerving drunk
& deviant
with a billion bones
on board.

there are no brakes!

the street curbs
& rails know
what the crash
feels like
before it tosses
us upside
down,

but we
can't hear
them scream

& we can't
see their
arms shake
erratically.

we just ride
deaf & blind,

smiling like fools
with lap belts on.

Voyeur

all
the street
lights
shine
while
the
grasshoppers
make
love,
&
i am
now
drunk
with
envy.

It's Worse in Wintertime

never feel
that your
mistress
sits &
waits for
your return
to her.

she lives
her life.

when the
hands of
the clock
reach your
time with
her, then
be on time,
& use the
time wisely,

otherwise
the hands
will continue
to tick away
seconds,
minutes,
& hours
that don't

involve you.
they all
add up to
days
that will
rip your
guts out
if you
believe
that
you are
the only one.

my stomach
has been
stitched,
& stapled
many times
over,
but that was
from the
early years.

now there
are just
scars, &
a clearer
understanding.

we are
strangers
in a crowd,
& lovers

otherwise.
it's a story
most people
will never
understand,
& those
that attempt
to,

know that
each time
you read
the story,

you close the
book with a
different
understanding.

it's
subjective,
but so is
poetry,

& there are
days which they
both feel like
a noose—
throbbing below my ears.

I Open The Screen Door & Scream

the
falling
snow
outside
beats
back my
freedom
like a
drunken
lover
that i
no longer
desire
to be
with,

or be without.

1 Bathroom in a
House full of Women

i hear
crickets
in the
bushes
& they
hear me.

they sing
so glorious
as i piss away
three, or four
beers
on a decent
tuesday night.

i shake
myself off
& zip up
on the
front steps.

i tell them,

"sing little
crickets,"

& they do.

           things are
looking up.

the winter chills
have passed,

& we are all damn grateful.

We are not Living

i have died
before
i was born.

i have died
on park benches
& in
crowded
christmas
shopping malls.

i have died
at the
kitchen sink
with soap
suds on my
hands.

i have died
before the morning coffee
finished perking.

i have died
reading
plath
with a
wine bottle
between my legs.

i have died
in mexican restaurants

with
fajitas
uneaten.

i have died
making love
with ex-
wives.

i have died
with
eastwood's
eyes &
curveballs.

i have died
with
a rose's
thorn in
my
hand.

i have died
in many
other
dreams
but,

i always
wake
alive,

& that is dying too.

She Just Thinks They Are Cute

there is a stray dog
that runs these blocks
& he is black with
long legs.

yesterday we watched him
chase a fat squirrel.

"do something!" she said,
"it's going to kill the
poor thing!"

"that is life," i told her.

she punched my shoulder
& stood up shouting,
"STOP GOD DAMN IT! STOP!"

the squirrel ran up a tree
& perched
with its stomach flapping
over both sides
of the small branch.

she stood up grabbing a rock
& threw it.

her aim is decent, but she
bounced it
three hops to the left.

the dog gave up & walked back
towards an alley.

she smiled satisfied
& walked back into the house
as i watched the squirrel
escape alive.

i have been that squirrel before:
pulse throbbing in my neck
& stuck
in moments that i had no clue
if i could survive.

the excitement was over
& i went back inside too.

we ordered chinese food:
rice, tangy chicken, noodles,
& egg drop.

we both got full
& she ran herself
some hot bathwater.

she climbed in
& i took all the leftovers
to the curb.

i like that dog.

i have been that dog before too.

We All Learn the Hard Way

i watched
the
black dog
again,
the one
with
long legs.

he had
a new
bitch
with
him
today.

she was
black
too,
& her
legs
were short.

they
walked
side
by side
making

stupid
looks
with their
lips.

the
streets
will eat
him alive
now,

tire
treads
to the
head
won't
hurt
as bad
as what
he has
coming.

he found
love.

Sometimes it Takes Moments like This to Remain a Man

i stumble into
the kitchen
& pull a
black handled
knife from
the drawer which
has many other
knives in it.

i pull the
cutting board
from the drawer
right below it
& toss it
onto the
kitchen table.

i'm drunk &
pulling my balls
out.

i'm lighting a
cigarette &
shouting,

"TAKE IT LIKE
A CHAMP!"

it's all dramatic,

& nobody gives
two shits.

i quickly realize
this & silence
my lips,

tuck my balls back
in,

zip up,

& laugh at the world.

The Road to Hell

a 70 mile journey at 16 miles
per hour; the road to hell was
snow packed & polished hot.

an enchanting melody played
on the radio,
& played on the radio,
played on the radio,
the radio.

the radio was stuck on repeat
& i feared that this journey
would be as well.
16 miles per hour.......
37 miles per hour.......
56 miles per hour.......
84 miles per hour.......
107 miles per hour.....
& the 70 mile journey now
gets shorter & shorter.

a finger of danger has started
to tickle me. i'll be to hell soon.

when i get there, i'll throw open
the door, toss my discarded objects
into a corner, pull the chain across
the locking mechanism & smile falsely,
muttering,
"hey baby, how was your day?
i could not wait to come home to you."

& Still Nobody Listens

you gotta find
                your beauty early—

take a blade in the guts for it,
buy it nice things on Friday nights:
spit, shit, & suck with it,
shower clean with it, take a
picture of it, write about it,
have a few good years with it,
loose it, & then search for it
again before it is too late, but

always remember—

yes, you may find it again, but
it will have turned with age &
it is just the way it goes;
it gets dull, it gets drab, & it
never returns the same.

it's a stranger, & now you just
have to find ways to satisfy the
days that are remaining with it:
mow its weeds, walk with crutches,
feed it medication, comb its hair,
wash the corner of its eyes,

lie to it,

& just hope that someone else
has given a goddamn that you are
alive, before you are dead.

Consumed

pulling up a pair
of twice before
worn jeans,
i found
$11. 83
in the pocket.

(moments like this are nice)

i'm going to spend it
on a bottle
of memories,

get drunk again,

& draw
pictures of the
most amazing
eyes all over
my walls.

it's odd, but

brandy
still does
these crazy
things to my
insides, &

i feel it when i am sober too.

Save the Spectacle for Someone Else

let them live.

let them prick
your fingers.

let the snakes
seek shelter in
the gardens.

let the bees suck
madly.

let them become
overgrown.

i ask of you.

when the moment
urges you,

do not cut the
flowers
to mourn me.

i would never
for you.

Thoughts with My Morning Beer

men
are complicated.

women
are complicated.

religions
are complicated.

governments
are complicated.

they try to prove all their
simplicities & superiority
through wars.

wars
are complicated.

cockroaches are simple,

& have laughed at humans for centuries.

I Concede Shortly Thereafter

she would shout,
& then open the front
door to remind me what
the feeling of fright
felt like.

Victor Clevenger spends his days in a Madhouse and his nights writing. Selected pieces of his work have appeared in print magazines and journals around the world. He is the author of several collections of poetry and together with American poet John Dorsey, they run *River Dog*. He can be reached at: crownofcrows@yahoo.com

This project was made possible, in part, by generous support from the Osage Arts Community.

Osage Arts Community provides temporary time, space and support for the creation of new artistic works in a retreat format, serving creative people of all kinds — visual artists, composers, poets, fiction and nonfiction writers. Located on a 152-acre farm in an isolated rural mountainside setting in Central Missouri and bordered by ¾ of a mile of the Gasconade River, OAC provides residencies to those working alone, as well as welcoming collaborative teams, offering living space and workspace in a country environment to emerging and mid-career artists. For more information, visit us at www.osageac.org

Osage Arts Community